# WHAT OTHERS ARE SAYING
## ABOUT THIS BOOK

*Glimpsing Eternity* is a thought-provoking work that examines profound gospel concepts in a way that makes them understandable. The liberal use of stories from both personal experiences and scripture provides wonderful illustrations that make complex gospel principles easier to understand and apply. The overarching theme of the book looks at how the conditions of our mortal existence operate within a constrained reality that exists within the larger reality of God's plan for each of his children. Examining several aspects of what this means to us is enlightening and well worth the time spent in this book.

—Scott Lloyd, healthcare executive and former bishop

A thoroughly enjoyable and stimulating book for those who appreciate pondering deeply the beauties of the gospel. In every chapter we felt we were in the company of a trusted, spiritual friend who brought new insights to eternal principles. We highly recommend this book.

—Richard and Ann Ray, stake patriarch

In his book, *Glimpsing Eternity*, Dwight Monson beautifully weaves his personal stories with the scriptures to answer the questions Latter-day Saints are confronted with today. Lifelong member, recent convert, investigator, or nonmember will each find divine truth in this book and will come to understand "things as they really are." With this knowledge and understanding, readers will be more prepared to embrace, teach, and defend eternal truth.

—Mark Quinn, stake patriarch

I have been reading *Glimpsing Eternity* and don't want to put it down. It is so beautifully written. I love the way it brings together both scripture and present-day examples. The real life stories and examples throughout the book are compelling and illustrate the insights perfectly! I hope that someday I can have a funeral service like Mrs. A.

—Dean Hales, president of the Centerville
Chapter of the Sons of the Utah Pioneers

Monson writes and thinks clearly. Each sentence and thought draws the reader to seek out the next one. His opening words make one want to read more, and when we did, we continued to want more. *Glimpsing Eternity* is relevant and valuable to anyone who likes thoughtful analysis of life and the way we can experience it. We must confess a bias since this is not the first Monson book we have read, and we're partial to his clear, compelling, and convincing style. We recommend this book. It is insightful and informative even for a Church member of many years.

—Bud & Mary Corkin, entrepreneurs
and missionaries extraordinaire

With the philosophies of men overwhelming our public—and even religious discourse—this book cuts through many of the alleged inequalities of the world to illustrate how God truly works and that He is, above all things, a just and loving God.

—Garrett Hall, lawyer and entrepreneur

# GLIMPSING

## Eternity

# GLIMPSING

## THINGS AS THEY REALLY ARE

# DWIGHT E. MONSON

CFI

An imprint of Cedar Fort, Inc.

Springville, Utah

This is not an official publication of The Church of Jesus Christ of Latter-day Saints. The opinions and views expressed herein belong solely to the author and do not necessarily represent the opinions or views of Cedar Fort, Inc. Permission for the use of sources, graphics, and photos is also solely the responsibility of the author.

ISBN 13: 978-1-4621-3701-5

Published by CFI, an imprint of Cedar Fort, Inc.
2373 W. 700 S., Springville, UT 84663
Distributed by Cedar Fort, Inc., www.cedarfort.com

Library of Congress Control Number: 2020933660

Cover design by Shawnda T. Craig
Cover design © 2020 Cedar Fort, Inc.

Printed in the United States of America

10 9 8 7 6 5 4 3 2 1

Printed on acid-free paper

# DEDICATION

To my beloved wife, Marilynn Allred Monson. You continue to inspire me to be a better man and a more devoted disciple of the Lord Jesus Christ. As you know, I am still a work in process, but thank you for your patient love and encouragement.

# OTHER INSIGHTFUL BOOKS BY DWIGHT MONSON

*Shared Beliefs, Honest Differences: A Biblical Basis for Comparing the Doctrines of Mormons and Other Christians*

*Understanding the LDS Temple: Experiencing God's Love*

# CONTENTS

CONTENTS

# INTRODUCTION

# TRUTH: THINGS AS THEY ARE

# CHAPTER 1

# WHAT IS TRUTH?

I T WAS MARK TWAIN WHO OBSERVED, "IT'S NOT THE THINGS WE don't know that get us into trouble. It's the things we know that just ain't so" (Goodreads.com). In this post-modern world of growing secularism, skepticism and relativism, members of The Church of Jesus Christ of Latter-day Saints must appear naïve and narrowminded to many as we stand forth boldly, proclaiming we know precious truths.

Latter-day Saints are blessed with additional scripture providing the Lord's definition of truth as found in D&C 93:24: "And truth is knowledge of things as they are, and as they were, and as they are to come."

The Lord's definition of truth implies key elements of God's great plan of happiness for His children. Truth is not limited to what we experience in this mortal realm with its unique conditions, a "sphere in which God has placed [us]" (D&C 93:30). Truth was truth before this earth rolled into existence, before Adam and Eve were placed in the garden, before mortality entered this fallen world. For eons before this mortal existence, truth was truth, and truth will continue through the long-anticipated millennium, through the Resurrection and Final Judgment, and through future eons of eternity.

Science employs a far-reaching assumption that things as we observe them today have always operated under the same laws and conditions and will continue to do so for the indefinite future. By contrast, we know from the revelations of God that this world is a fallen world, far different from the paradisiacal conditions in which it once operated, and even more different from the highest degree of glory that is its destiny.

One of the conditions of this fallen sphere, in the words of the Apostle Paul, is that "now we see through a glass darkly . . . now [we] know in part" (1 Corinthians 13:12). It would seem only reasonable that "things as they are, and as they were, and as they are to come" are, in fact, different from what we perceive from our constrained vantage point.

One of the great stories in the Old Testament illustrates this very principle. It is found in 2 Kings 6:8–18. To summarize, the king of Syria was frustrated in his efforts to defeat the Israelites in battle because the prophet Elisha kept revealing Syrian designs so the Israelites could escape and successfully defend themselves. The king of Syria called a council of his leaders, asserting that one of them must be betraying their plans to the enemy. After much frantic discussion, one of the Syrian leaders suggested the problem was instead due to the intervention of the Israelite prophet, Elisha. The king ordered spies to find Elisha so they could apprehend him. Elisha was located in Dothan and surrounded by a great host of warriors on horses and chariots. Early in the morning, Elisha's servant arose, and perceiving their desperate situation, he informed his master, "Alas . . . how shall we do?" Elisha's response was, "Fear not: for they that be with us are more than they that be with them."

The account continues, "And Elisha prayed, and said, Lord, I pray thee open his eyes that he may see. And the Lord opened the eyes of the young man; and he saw: and behold the mountain was full of horses and chariots of fire round about . . . And Elisha prayed . . . Smite this people, I pray thee, with blindness. And [the Lord] smote them with blindness according to the word of Elisha" (2 Kings 6:15–18).

It is important to note that both Elisha and his servant were fully cognizant of real danger. The reality of this world, in this case, the Syrian army, was clear and unmistakable. But this story beautifully demonstrates a profound truth; namely, *the conditions of our mortal existence operate within a constrained reality that exists within a larger reality.* Though the temporal forces of the Syrian army were actual and great, there was a larger reality that Elisha was able to access, and he prayed that the servant might see it also and not fear. Elisha understood that the very real threat posed by the amassed army did not comprise the totality of their situation. In the larger reality, Elisha perceived correctly that "they that be with us are more than they that be with them." This larger reality did not invalidate the temporal reality of the Syrian army, but it completely altered the outcome of what ensued.

And so it is with us. We live each day in a very real world of constrained reality that operates within a larger reality. We call this reality the economy of God. And when we access this larger reality, we see things more completely: as they are, as they were, and as they are to come. Then, in the words of Paul, we will "look not at the things which are seen, but at the things which are not seen: for the things which are seen are temporal; but the things which are not seen are eternal" (2 Corinthians 4:18).

This book is an attempt to describe various aspects of how God's economy operates, altering outcomes in the "seen" world and enabling all to access the power of an "unseen" world that eludes us when we limit our view to a temporal perspective with all its constraints.

# SECTION I
# AN ABUNDANT LIFE

# CHAPTER 2

# SCARCITY AND ABUNDANCE

PERHAPS THE MOST PERSISTENT AND PERVASIVE CONSTRAINED reality we encounter in this temporal world is scarcity. In economics, the law of scarcity can be expressed simply as infinite wants meet finite resources.

For example, there will never be sufficient gold to satisfy all of its desired uses by all people. Ironically, if there were, its value would plummet to near zero. It is, in fact, scarcity that gives gold its high value, and when it becomes more or less scarce, it becomes more or less valuable.

Another example is bottled water. Who could have foreseen fifty years ago that pure, drinkable water would become sufficiently scarce that people would willingly pay a dollar or more for a twelve-ounce bottle of water? Back then, the availability of water with desirable properties was held to be so abundant that people would have thought it a joke to offer water even at ten cents per bottle. What changed is our perception of scarcity and, with it, perceptions of value.

By contrast, in God's economy, what is valued and of greatest worth is found in abundance. For example, in God's economy, there is no constraint on the number who can attain eternal life; no finite, predetermined limit; no bell-shaped grading curve; no competition with few winners and many losers. Rather, all who abide the law upon which the blessing of celestial glory is predicated will attain exaltation (D&C 88:38–39; 130:20–21). All are invited to partake freely of all that the Father has. The Savior extends His invitation: "Come unto me all ye ends of the earth, buy milk and honey, without money and without price" (2 Nephi 26:25). Each child of God born into mortality is capable of enlargement and progression, grace by grace (see *Teachings of the Prophet Joseph Smith*, 354, and D&C 93:20). Eternal life, "the greatest of all the gifts of God" (D&C 14:7), is available in abundance.

Providentially, we see glimpses of the reality of abundance in our constrained world. For instance, a case can be made that love is the most highly desired commodity in the world. This is evident in how consistently it appears in music, literature, and the arts in all forms. It is the foundation of a happy childhood, and its absence is likely to create neuroses and dysfunctional behavior at any stage of life. It is a universal "good" in every belief system.

One of the wonderful properties of love, even in our constrained world, is the lack of limits on the amount of love one person can possess. So when a mother of one beloved child bears her second, the love she feels for the first is not diminished or divided. Rather, a mother's love is capable of growing and expanding exponentially to include an additional child and to feel even greater love as she encounters the uniqueness of each in contrast to the other. Love knows no intrinsic bounds or limits, only those of our own creation and choosing.

The reality of abundance in this constrained existence is also evident in the law of tithing. Everyone acknowledges that a dollar less ten cents leaves only ninety cents, a zero-sum game in which a 10 percent loss always results. However, the Lord has invited us to experience His abundance. "Prove me now herewith, saith the Lord of hosts, if I will not open you the windows of heaven, and pour you out a blessing, that there shall not be room enough to receive it" (Malachi 3:10).

Many tithe-payers, both Latter-day Saints and others, can attest to an abundant reality that accompanies the law of tithing. Despite the very real 10 percent reduction in resources, faithful tithe-payers recognize a gain that exceeds their sacrifice. In the payment of tithes, Elisha's response to his servant finds a parallel: "Fear not: for the resources provided by the Lord . . . are more than the resources paid in tithes."

This principle of abundance amidst scarcity is beautifully illustrated in the story of another Old Testament prophet, Elijah. He had been commanded to pronounce the heavens closed, ushering in a prolonged drought. To save his life, the Lord eventually directed Elijah to a widow in the city of Zarephath, where he found her gathering sticks to bake a last morsel of bread. With only a handful of flour and a little oil, she was preparing a final meal for her son and herself, thereafter expecting to perish from want of food.

> And Elijah said unto her, Fear not; go and do as thou hast said, but make me thereof a little cake first and bring it to me, and after make for thee and for thy son. For thus saith the Lord God of Israel, The barrel of meal shall not waste, neither shall the cruse of oil fail, until the day that the Lord sendeth rain upon the earth. And she went and did according to the word of Elijah; and she and he and her house, did eat many days. (1 Kings 17:13–15)

The widow's situation could not have been bleaker. The reality of scarce food brought on by the drought was evident to both Elijah and the widow, but exercising faith, she put God first by feeding the Lord's servant before tending to her own needs, and the Lord provided abundance to sustain her and her house until the drought subsided.

The actuality of abundance in a constrained world is not only attested to in sacred writ. It is also evident in the most basic principles of farming: sowing seeds. Who was it that concluded tossing precious grain into the earth would bring forth a bountiful harvest? On the face of it, this act made no more sense than the one performed by the widow, but in this exercise of faith that we take for granted today, the law of abundance is clearly manifest. "For the earth is full, and there is enough and to spare, yea, I [the Lord] prepared all things . . . take of the abundance which I have made" (D&C 104:17–18).

Likewise, in his groundbreaking book, *Think and Grow Rich*, Napoleon Hill identified seventeen principles for attaining wealth, as well as other worthy goals. He described how wealth appears so elusive until it reveals itself after application of what Hill calls the laws of success. Hill writes, "When Riches begin to come, they come so quickly and in such great abundance that one wonders where they have been hiding during all those lean years" (*Think and Grow Rich*, 8). According to Hill, abundance is always present, but it does not present itself until one applies the principles upon which such blessings are predicated. Then it is as if one's eyes are opened to the abundant reality that was always there but was obscured by our constrained perspective.

Another example can be seen in finite oil reserves found on this planet. In 1956, M. King Hubert authored an oft-cited treatise called *Nuclear Energy and the Fossil Fuels*, which forecasted worldwide oil production trends. Based on known reserves, Hubert predicted oil production would peak in the early 2000s, declining steadily thereafter. While it is ultimately true that there is a finite amount of oil reserves on earth, Hubert's projections have proven woefully inaccurate because huge new reserves have been discovered and advances in technology have expanded the ability to produce much more oil from existing wells. In 1956, known oil reserves totaled 1.2 trillion barrels. Today, after more than fifty years of increasing consumption, known oil reserves stand at 1.6 trillion barrels, 33 percent more than when Hubert prepared his estimate.

In his newsletter dated September 12, 2012, investment advisor Porter Stansberry commented on these developments:

Look around. Observe that the same kind of abundance tends to manifest itself in almost every area of human endeavor. The simple fact is, the more energy we use, the more we discover. Likewise, the more computers we make, the better they get. The more food we grow, the more efficiently we can grow it. This so-called experience curve is the result of the application of the human mind. (*Stansberry's Investment Advisory*)

It is also the result of an abundance that operates in God's economy and supersedes the limits of a constrained reality we often perceive as intractable in our temporal existence.

# CHAPTER 3

# THE MEASURE OF GREATNESS

MOHAMMAD ALI, THE BOXING LEGEND, PROCLAIMED TO THE world, "I am the greatest," and by some measures, perhaps he was in his chosen profession. With his flamboyant personality, the Louisville Lip, as he was affectionately dubbed, transcended the boxing scene onto a world stage, while defeating worthy champions including Sonny Liston, Smokin' Joe Frazier, Ken Norton, and George Foreman. By the standards of the world, he was great; maybe even the greatest.

In the constrained reality of this world, the number of those who achieve such distinction is necessarily limited. Mohammad Ali takes his place with other distinguished figures such as Albert Einstein, William Shakespeare, Martin Luther King Jr., and Michelangelo, to name a few. Our popular culture glamorizes such celebrity in annual lists of the most influential, the wealthiest, the most beautiful, the best athletes, the most famous, and so on.

By contrast, when the Savior found His disciples disputing among themselves "who should be the greatest," He taught, "Ye know that the princes of the Gentiles exercise dominion over them and they that are great exercise authority upon them. But it shall not be so among you: but whosoever will be great among you, let him be the minister; And whosoever will be chief among you, let him be your servant" (Matthew 20:25–27). In God's economy, the measure of greatness is service and goodness directed toward others. Opportunities for excelling in service and goodness are abundant and unconstrained.

Peter's one line tribute of His master reveals the distilled essence of godlike greatness: "Jesus . . . went about doing good" (Acts 10:38). He healed, He taught, He ministered, and He served. He organized and built the kingdom of God on earth and then atoned for the sins of the world. As was said of another, his life was "abundant in goodness" (Exodus 34:6). Nephi foretold, "He doeth not anything save it be for the benefit of the world; for he loveth the world, even that he layeth down his own life" (2 Nephi 26:24).

Is goodness really the measure of greatness, or is this a rationalization that lowers the bar so mediocre individuals can feel good about their undistinguished lives as espoused by some and suspected by many? The recent experience of a dear family friend provides perspective and opens eyes to a larger reality.

My friend, we shall call her Sarah, is an older woman who loves to entertain and enjoys sharing her cooking talents with friends and neighbors. Regularly, she invites individuals and couples from her church and neighborhood into her home for dinner or family home evenings. However, one couple in the neighborhood was never invited. They are less social than most, perhaps self-conscious of tattoos, limited education, and at times awkward mannerisms. For these reasons, Sarah told herself it was not necessary to reach out.

One day, Sarah's three-wheel bicycle was stolen out of her garage in broad daylight. After sharing her loss with several neighbors in hopes they might have observed something or someone, she contacted a local bike store and was disappointed when informed how much it would cost to replace the stolen bike. She decided she could not afford it and moved on with her daily routine.

A few weeks later, a knock came at her door. When she opened it, Sarah was surprised to find the wife of this less-social couple. This woman explained that she had heard of the stolen bike and of the expense involved in replacing it. She had contacted Sarah's neighbors as well as members of their church. This woman told how neighbors and friends had responded generously, contributing funds to replace the bike.

Sarah was flabbergasted and humbled. She had never invited this woman into her home, yet she was taking initiative to bless her life. In that moment of unexpected goodness, Sarah's perceptions of her and her husband changed instantaneously. Sarah was no longer concerned with their limitations, be they social, educational, or anything else. None of that mattered, because this woman's goodness overwhelmed all other considerations. She immediately attained a stature in Sarah's mind that would never again relegate her to ordinary or unexceptional. Sarah saw the nobility of this woman's spirit and her greatness in goodness.

Sarah's experience can be generalized to all through a little exercise in self-reflection, sometimes attributed to the Peanuts cartoon creator, Charles Schultz. Ask yourself this set of questions: Can you name the five wealthiest individuals in the world? The last three Heisman trophy winners? The last three winners of the Nobel Prize for literature? Next, ask yourself the following: Can you name two teachers who made a difference in your education? Three friends who helped you through a difficult time? Five people who have made a difference in your life and your values?

The initial list comprises first-rate achievers, but their accomplishments fade and pale in comparison to the goodness wrought by more ordinary people who will always be great to you because of their impact on your life.

In a related vein, the story is told of when King George III asked American-born painter Benjamin West what General George Washington planned to do now that he had won the war. West replied, "They say he will return to his farm." King George said, "If he does that, he will be the greatest man in the world" (Paul Johnson, *George Washington: The Founding Father*, and David Boaz, "The Man Who Would Not Be King").

King George's response is intriguing in part, because it is so counter-intuitive. According to the King, Washington would be the greatest man in the world if he walked away from power, position, and distinction. Yet, these are the very qualities that our constrained world extols and elevates. Occupying the pinnacle of world power, King George III perhaps understood better than most the true measure of a man's greatness.

In the community of St. George, Utah, a few old-timers still occasionally recount the story about the funeral of Mrs. A. This diminutive woman passed away at the age of sixty-two, having dealt with persistent health problems on and off in her life. She never held a prominent position in her church or community, but she found a way of serving many, many people through her gift of excellent cooking. Her husband owned a business that brought him in contact with many people in St. George. Each day he would report to his wife: Mrs. So-and-so is ill or this-or-that family is struggling. Though the family's means were modest, they had access to low-cost food through Mr. A's business. Each day as Mrs. A prepared food for her large family, she made an extra pan of casserole, baked three extra loaves of bread, or a couple dozen extra cookies for those in need of a little kindness and care. She sent her children on their bikes to deliver the food with a message: "We're thinking about you today and hope you feel better."

So on an unusually cold and damp January evening in St. George, people lined up for hours, the queue extending for blocks, to pay tribute to Mrs. A and her family. Hours of the viewing were extended late into the night, but finally people had to be turned away. They were invited to return the next day beginning at an hour much earlier than previously announced when the viewing would continue. The next morning the lines extended again for blocks and still everyone was not able to pay their respects before the funeral services commenced much later than originally planned.

The funeral director had recently relocated to St. George from Salt Lake City. He remarked, "I have been involved in funerals for dignitaries, including governors and prominent church leaders, but I have never seen anything like this." (The son of Mrs. A related this account to the author.) Those holding high office can never compete for the affection of people served so consistently and thoughtfully through the goodness of one like Mrs. A.

Imagine a world in which humans set their minds and hearts on goodness toward others instead of competing for limited wealth, fame, power, and distinction. Envision a world where national leaders are honored only for their service to the common good. Like other divine attributes, there is no constraint on the abundance of greatness such goodness would produce.

CHAPTER 4

# THE SACRED AND THE PROFANE

IN HIS DREAM, THE PROPHET LEHI BEHELD A GREAT AND SPACIOUS building, symbolizing the institutions of man with worldly power, wealth, and position. The people inside "were in the attitude of mocking and pointing their fingers toward those who were partaking of the fruit" (1 Nephi 8:27). Today, we see this attitude in many segments of society: belittling belief in God, making light of moral values, and ridiculing ideas others consider sacred. Those who protest are often branded as prudish and intolerant. Truly, Lehi foresaw our day depicted in his dream.

Despite such opposition, the Lord expects us to respect the sacred and reverence the sublime.

As one General Authority has observed, "Our ability to seek, recognize and reverence the holy above the profane, and the sacred above the secular, defines our spirituality" (Dennis B. Neuenschwander, "Holy Place, Sacred Space").

One way we reverence the holy is to use discretion in sharing sacred, personal experiences. The prophet Alma taught, "It is given unto many to know the mysteries of God; they are laid under a strict command that they shall not impart only according to the portion of his word which he doth grant" (Alma 12:9). In our day, President Marion G. Romney counseled, "I do not tell all I know . . . for I found out that if I talked too lightly of sacred things, thereafter the Lord would not trust me" (counsel given to mission presidents and

19

their wives in Geneva, Switzerland, June 25, 1982; cited by Boyd K. Packer in "The Candle of the Lord").

Most often, what we encounter in this life consists of the common and mundane, but the Lord and His servants have provided guideposts to aid us in distinguishing the holy from the ordinary. With spiritual discernment, we perceive things as they really are in God's economy, allowing us to distinguish the sacred amid the profane in this temporal sphere.

For example, when living prophets counsel youth to reject tattoos and body piercings, some may be inclined to discount or trivialize such teachings. After all, aren't the youth of today faced with more daunting challenges? However, the Apostle Paul wrote, "For the temple of God is holy, which temple ye are" (1 Corinthians 3:17). With the same respect we show for the House of the Lord, we should embrace the wisdom of treating the human body as the temple it is.

Similarly, procreative powers are increasingly depicted in popular culture as a natural act between consenting adults that harms no one, providing pleasure and self-gratification. Such a perspective seems to ignore the all-too-common, temporal consequences: STDs, broken homes and fractured relationships, single-parent poverty, unwanted pregnancies, and conscience-deadening abortions. It also belies the sublime and sacred nature of this gift from God, as illustrated in an experience with a former business colleague. We will call him Jason.

Jason was married to a believer, not of the LDS faith, who fervently wished her husband shared her belief in God, if not her religion. For Jason's part, he described himself as "agnostic on a good day." As the delivery of their first baby approached, I shared with Jason spiritual impressions I felt at the birth of my children, encouraging him to be sensitive to manifestations of the spirit in the moments surrounding birth. A week or two later, I received a call from Jason, sharing the good news of their baby girl's arrival. Then Jason's voice transitioned from excitement to a humble, somber tone. He simply stated, "I found God in the delivery room."

With perspective born of the spirit, we realize procreation is much more than passion and pleasure. In intimate moments, we become one with another child of God, spirit touching spirit. Later, at birth, procreation becomes a sacred partnership with Deity to populate this world, in similitude of the powers of godliness that bring forth spirit sons and daughters. As such, procreative powers are so holy they should be used only within parameters ordained by the Lord: abstinence outside of marriage, total fidelity in marriage. Few things are more important to our spirituality than how we deal with these God-given powers. We honor their sacred nature by exercising them within bounds the Lord has set.

Of course, this is not easy or without sacrifice. The natural man in us sees obedience to God's commandments as restrictive, even repressive. However, with wisdom and experience, it becomes clear that all of God's commandments constitute a loving revelation of laws upon which enduring happiness is predicated; a source of blessing and protection. The Lord's "commandments are spiritual; they are not natural, nor temporal, neither carnal nor sensual" (D&C 29:35). Accordingly, blessings brought forth by obedience to God's laws are also spiritual, and "The fruit of the Spirit is love, joy, peace, longsuffering, gentleness, goodness, faith, meekness, temperance" (Galatians 5:22–23). In God's economy, obedience in emulation of the Savior's life constitutes the apex of spirituality and the most sublime form of worship.

For this reason, it is not sufficient to simply recognize the sacred, but we are also expected to demonstrate appropriate reverence through our actions. For example, a few years ago, our family lived in a stake where one of its members possessed the sixteenth copy of the Book of Mormon printed in 1829. The owner kept this precious volume wrapped in a towel, and when displayed, he took precautions to make certain no human hands touched it. However, as valuable as this rare book is, its enduring value lies in its words and far exceeds the book's temporal worth. Accordingly, the appropriate way to demonstrate respect for the sacred nature of the Book of Mormon is to drink deeply and often from its pages.

Just as we show respect for volumes of holy scripture by wearing them out, we demonstrate reverence for the sacred privilege of communing with our Father in Heaven by engaging in daily solemn prayers and careful pondering. Likewise, we evidence our appreciation for the temple by visiting it often, regularly accessing the power of the Spirit to enlighten and edify us.

The same is true for reverencing the gift of repentance and the Atonement of Jesus Christ. We show respect for His supernal grace by calling upon its powers to heal us daily. President Boyd K. Packer has observed,

For some reason, we think the Atonement of Christ applies *only* at the end of mortal life, to redemption from the Fall, from spiritual death. It is much more than that. It is an ever-present power to call upon in everyday life. When we are racked or harrowed up or tormented by guilt or burdened with grief, He can heal us. . . . We can experience "the peace of God, which passeth all understanding." (Boyd K. Packer, "Touch of the Master's Hand")

For the Atonement to have practical value, one must apply it in his or her life on an ongoing basis.

This is particularly true when grappling with grievous sins. Our temporal minds tend to harbor poignant memories, beating us up and not allowing us to let go of the past. However, the Lord has informed us, "Behold, he who has repented of his sins, the same is forgiven, and I, the Lord, remember them no more" (D&C 58:42). With understanding of the Atonement as it operates in God's economy, we will move forward with hope and faith, trusting in His precious blood to make us pure. "Though your sins be as scarlet, they shall be white as snow; though they be red like crimson, they shall be as wool" (Isaiah 1:18).

I recall from my youth the analogy of a nail driven into a pristine board. After extracting the nail, a hole remains. We can fill it with wood filler, sand it, stain it, or apply other treatments, but the mark is still visible upon close examination. As our temporal minds recall past indiscretions, we too often focus attention, as it were, on marks still visible in our board of life. In those moments of self-incrimination, we should reverence the absolute healing powers of the Atonement. The miracle of the Atonement is not that Christ fills the holes left by our sins. Rather, the miracle of the Atonement in God's economy is that the board is restored to its perfect, pristine state.

We show respect for the sacred gift of the Atonement by repenting of our sins daily and by partaking of the sacrament each Sunday, renewing our determination to endure in its power. Thus, we seek, recognize, and reverence the holy above the profane and the sacred above the secular in the most precious of all God's gifts in this life.

# SECTION II
# ETERNAL PROGRESSION

# CHAPTER 5

# THE MORAL LAW

As JOHN ADAMS FAMOUSLY ASSERTED, "FACTS ARE STUBBORN things; and whatever may be our wishes, our inclinations, or the dictates of our passions, they cannot alter the state of facts and evidence" (Brainyquote.com). While honest seekers of truth subscribe to different bodies of thought in explaining the origins of human existence, all parties agree that physical laws operate across the universe. With few exceptions, observable systems of physical phenomena are structured and orderly. For example, two parts hydrogen combined with one part oxygen produce liquid water, which turns into a solid mass at 32 degrees Fahrenheit and vaporous gas at 212 degrees. The orderly operation of physical laws results in observable facts, making them difficult to dispute and ignore, or in Adam's words: "stubborn things."

Scripture informs us that God structured our temporal world to operate by laws (D&C 88:13; 93:30). In fact, the operation of law is so central to God's economy that without it "there could have been no creation of things, neither to act nor to be acted upon" (2 Nephi 2:13). Likewise, if God were to violate His own laws, He would cease to be God (Alma 42:12, 22). Our God honors and abides laws and covenants unwaveringly. It is a defining characteristic of godliness.

God's laws not only define the parameters within which our physical world operates. They also reveal how the Gods interact with one another and with us, and how we should treat our fellow human beings. Commandments and righteous covenants are a revelation of how God lives and of how we should conduct our lives so we can be like Him, dwell with Him, and receive all He has. These rules constitute the moral law, which operates perfectly in the economy of God and manifests itself with power in this temporal sphere.

As with physical laws, moral laws have predetermined consequences (D&C 82:4). The predictable result of sin is "punishment and misery" (2 Nephi 2:13). Likewise, the foreordained outcome of righteousness is lasting happiness and joy, "even peace in this world and eternal life in the world to come" (D&C 59:23).

Unlike many physical laws, however, some consequences of sin and righteousness are not readily apparent, so wickedness often appears to prosper in the short run, prompting the psalmist to lament, "Lord, how long shall the wicked triumph?" (Psalms 94:3; see also 73:12–14 and Jeremiah 12:1). Based on "things that are seen," the moral law often appears not to operate effectively in this temporal world.

However, this is an incomplete depiction of a larger reality. In that moment when agency meets temptation, we make choices that have unavoidable consequences. The light of Christ, which "lighteth every man that cometh into the world" (D&C 93:2), endows every one of us with the capacity to know good from evil (Moroni 7:16; Helaman 14:31). When we sin, we knowingly turn away from the light, and when we choose righteousness, we knowingly move toward it. Our minds may not consciously process the event, but our spirits perceive its effects unerringly.

Inevitably, rebellion is preceded by rationalization and self-justification, attempting to assuage the conscience. How vain and futile it is if we have "sought all the days of [our] lives for that which [we can] not obtain . . . for happiness in doing iniquity, which thing is contrary to the nature of righteousness" (Helaman 13:38). Over time, the conscience can become dulled and deadened to promptings of the spirit when consistently unheeded, but the moral law continues to operate on the spirit of man.

Such was the case with King David. Having first observed Bathsheba bathing from afar, he made inquiries as to her identity. Once informed that she was the wife of one of his loyal soldiers, Uriah the Hitite, he faced a decision to act on his lustful desires or to remain true to the Lord's commandment: Thou shalt not commit adultery. David knowingly turned from the light, sending messengers to take her so he could lie with her. Later when she became pregnant with his child, he was confronted with another set of options. Rather than repenting and confessing his sins, he attempted to hide them, first by bringing Uriah back from the battlefront and ultimately conspiring to have him killed (2 Samuel 11).

At each crucial decision point, King David convinced himself that his actions were somehow justified. In the process, his sensitivity to things of the spirit dulled until his conscience was oblivious to the depths of his iniquity. The conspicuous injustice of his actions only dawned on him when the Prophet Nathan related the tale of a poor man whose one little ewe was appropriated by a wealthy lord, refusing to use one of his own numerous sheep to provide his meal.

"And David's anger was greatly kindled against the (wealthy) man; and he said to Nathan, As the Lord liveth the man that hath done this thing shall surely die. . . . And Nathan said to David, Thou art the man" (2 Samuel 12:5, 7). Confronted with a different set of facts, the obvious injustice of King David's actions became apparent, but King David had become desensitized to the evil of his own choices until parallel events were presented involving different actors.

The scriptures refer to this process as hardening the heart. This is the inevitable consequence of persistent, unrepented sin. This same effect of deadening the soul is evident in Nephi's rebuke of his brothers: "Ye are swift to do iniquity but slow to remember the Lord your God. Ye have seen an angel, and he spake unto you; yea, ye have heard his voice from time to time; and he hath spoken unto you in a still small voice, but ye were past feeling, that you could not feel his words" (1 Nephi 17:45).

The operation of God's laws evokes an inescapable reaction in each of us every time we make moral choices. In this temporal existence, hearts and spirits either soften in humility and contrition or steel themselves against incessant pangs of conscience, without exception. There is no compromise, no third option, for "wickedness never was happiness" (Alma 41:10). It is one of those immutable facts established in God's wisdom, and "facts are stubborn things."

In God's wisdom, abiding the moral law inevitably produces natural consequences: peace and enduring joy (2 Nephi 2:13; Alma 41:16). The Savior assured His disciples, "Peace I leave with you, my peace I give unto you: not as the world giveth, give I unto you" (John 14:27). This peace is but one of the precious fruits of the spirit poured out on those who soften their hearts, turning from sin toward light (Galatians 5:22–23).

However, embracing the light does not solve all of life's challenges. Several years ago, our family witnessed the conversion of a dear sister that we will call Diane. Before joining the Church, Diane had significant family and financial problems. She also struggled with a word of wisdom habit that took its toll on her health. Entering the waters of baptism and receiving the gift of the Holy Ghost did not make these problems disappear. Six months after joining the Church, Diane confided that she was still struggling with most of the same challenges but that things were much better. This improvement was not due to her temporal circumstances but rather resulted from a peace in her life, giving her courage and fortitude to confront life's challenges with faith and confidence. Her peace was "not as the world giveth" but as the Savior promised.

This peace is a powerful and enduring blessing. A few years ago, I had the privilege of being the primary caregiver to my mother during the last four and one-half months of her life. As it became evident that she would soon pass through the veil, I talked with her about her life. When death draws near, pretense is forgotten. What really matters comes into focus with great clarity. Because of our human nature, no one gets through a long life without a few regrets, and Mom was no exception. I shall never forget the peace and serenity that pervaded her soul and bestowed deep joy in her dying hours. She had chosen wisely in the big decisions of life. She was supremely content, and, in her quiet demeanor, I beheld true success.

As the end of mortal life approaches, it is clear that success is not measured in wealth, fame, position, or honors of men. Rather, true success comes from knowing one's choices have made a real difference in the lives of those he or she loves most. Or, as another has written, "Success in life depends upon happiness, and happiness is found in no other way than through service that is rendered in a spirit of love" (Napoleon Hill, *Law of Success*, 128). God exemplifies this measure himself. His work and His glory is "to bring to pass the immortality and eternal life of man" (Moses 1:39), blessing sons and daughters He loves with a perfect love.

Because true success pertains to "things as they are, and as they were, and as they are to come," righteous choices not only bless our own lives in the present, but they also have the power to bless lives for generations to come. This can occur through our own faithful posterity as well as the posterity of those we assist in coming unto Christ in missionary efforts. Righteous choices also bless past generations through our righteous endeavors in genealogy and temple work.

In God's supernal goodness, He has provided a way to attain a fullness of joy for our loved ones and for us through the Atonement of Jesus Christ by making and keeping covenants to live His moral law. There is no other way. It is one of those stubborn things.

## CHAPTER 6

# AFFLICTIONS AND BLESSINGS

THE EPIC STORY OF JOB AS RECORDED IN THE OLD TESTAMENT contains many lessons that defy easy explanation without reference to the larger reality of God's economy. Some of these lessons are essential to making sense of mortality with its many challenges and opportunities.

As is well known, Job was a prosperous, upright man in whom the Lord took pleasure, but Satan insisted Job's righteousness was due to his comfortable circumstances, so the Lord permitted Satan to try Job in the crucible of affliction. In one day, Job lost his oxen, sheep, and camels. Then he lost all his sons and daughters. Job reacted most humbly. He said, "Naked came I out of my mother's womb, and naked shall I return thither: the Lord gave, and the Lord hath taken away; blessed be the name of the Lord" (Job 1:21).

Soon thereafter, Job was afflicted further. He was smitten with boils, and his face and body were disfigured. Friends came to console him, but their words only tormented him, which added insult to injury. His wife lost her faith and exhorted her husband, "Curse God, and die." Job responded, "What? Shall we receive good at the hand of God, and shall we not receive evil?" (Job 2:9, 10).

Through his trials, Job endured in righteousness, and, in time, his prior possessions were restored and more. He received a two-fold increase in livestock and was blessed with ten more sons and daughters to comfort him. Toward the end of his ordeal, Job was privileged to see the Lord with his own eyes and received "things too wonderful for me, which I knew not" (Job 42:2, 5). Job passed his test and received an eternal reward.

So all's well that ends well. Or is it?

The philosopher Friedrich Nietzsche observed that though justice may have ultimately been served for Job, such was not the case for his original posterity, not to mention the innocent livestock. From what is recorded, Job's first family of sons and daughters had done nothing to warrant sudden destruction, yet they were treated as pawns in the battle for Job's soul (C. J. Jung, *Nietzsche's Zarathustra*, 1050).

Similarly, one might question the entire process described in the book of Job. Was this drama really necessary and beneficial? After all, God is all-knowing and sees the end from the beginning. He did not need to agree to this charade to establish the integrity of Job's heart.

A similar line of inquiry might be extended to inexplicable horrors endured by many in this mortal sphere: Six million Jews slaughtered in the holocaust, an innocent child contracting virulent cancer, the suffering and deprivation of entire populations born into squalor and abject poverty. Are these horrors really necessary and beneficial in advancing God's purposes? Likewise, we all know of individuals with physical disabilities due to birth defects, untimely accidents, or persistent health issues; heartbreaking devastation resulting from premature death; wrenching divorce or heinous abuse; financial struggles and societal inequities. And the list goes on. Where is God's justice in this temporal existence? Or is the world really as cruel and absurd as it sometimes seems?

Only the restored gospel of Jesus Christ supplies fully satisfying answers to these and other challenging questions. Only "knowledge of things as they are, and as they were, and as they are to come" can provide context to make sense of life's troubling contradictions. Trying to explain the suffering and inequalities of mortality—without reference to our premortal existence, the purpose of this mortal probation and the eternal possibilities that await us—is like trying to divine the ending of a three-part play based entirely on performances in the second act. One can only conjure up wild guesses as to how dilemmas posed in the middle scenes came to be in the first place and how they will resolve themselves ultimately, if at all.

Amid personal trials in Liberty Jail, the Prophet Joseph Smith recorded an intimate revelation, providing deep insight into the larger reality required to make sense of mortal challenges. After recounting a litany of afflictions, most of which the Prophet had already endured, the Savior instructed His prophet, "Know this, my son, that all these things shall give thee experience, and shall be for thy good" (D&C 122:7–8).

Joseph was made to understand that this life is intended to be an intense learning and growing process, providing valuable "experience" that "shall be for thy good" (D&C 121:7). This counsel is similar to that given to Adam prior to being cast out of the Garden of Eden. "Cursed is the ground *for thy sake*" (Genesis 3:17; italics added). In both instances, the Lord describes trials as blessings that will be "for thy good" and "for thy sake." We can only glimpse such counter-intuitive truth through the lens of God's economy.

Author and speaker Peter Jeppson has related his own encounter with devastating challenges. When in his teens, Peter was involved in a tragic accident that resulted in third-degree burns over more than half of his body. Cartilage in his nose and ears was destroyed, leaving his face disturbingly disfigured. Simple functions such as blinking to lubricate eyes became nearly impossible. Pain and suffering were beyond comprehension for anyone who has not suffered a similar mishap.

While lying in his hospital bed, a young woman visited Peter nearly every day and read to him. It was clear her intentions were purely motivated out of compassion and kindly service. As Peter lay there, he realized how self-absorbed his life had been and how unlikely it was that he would have rendered such selfless service to another in similar circumstances.

Months after his accident, and while still struggling with his rehabilitation, Peter met with a General Authority of the Church who asked the following question: "Based on what you know, if you could choose, would you elect to suffer this tragedy?" The Church leader said he did not want Peter's answer immediately, but he requested that Peter return in a year and give his response. Peter's immediate reaction was outrage, appalled that anyone could be so insensitive and unfeeling to suggest someone would will such horrific conditions for himself. Yet, over the ensuing year, Peter grew in his realization of how this accident had completely transformed his character, softening him and making him much more loving, caring, and responsive to others. One year later, Peter reported back to the General Authority, declaring the changes in his character more than compensated for his suffering and ongoing challenges (Peter Jeppson, *The Peter Jeppson Story*).

Peter's amazing insight reflects a humble realization that his tragedy provided invaluable "experience," producing changes "for [his] good" and accelerating personal progression toward becoming like his Father in Heaven. If mortality, the second act, is the totality of the drama we call life, Peter's suffering would have been indeed tragic and senseless.

Knowledge of our premortal existence informs us that we all developed and progressed in our own unique way before coming to earth. Adversity and trials in this life serve the benevolent purpose of filling in gaps, of advancing our growth and development. "There must be opposition in all things . . . if not, righteousness could not be brought to pass . . . neither holiness . . . neither good" (2 Nephi 2:11). Redemption requires each of God's children to pass through an individualized course of instruction so he or she can progress.

Scripture informs us that we "shouted for joy" (Job 38:4–7) at the opportunity of coming to earth. The plan presented by a loving Heavenly Father included a description of life beyond the grave, an eternity in His presence filled with indescribable joy and glory. These precious promises assured us of rewards beyond mortal comprehension, more than justifying the price required to fill the gaps in our personal development so we can attain all the Father has, all He desires to share with us.

In that premortal state, each of us had full knowledge of the conditions and suffering of this life and some awareness of specific challenges and trials that awaited us. With faith and courage, we chose to pass through these experiences, knowing this course would ultimately bless us and be for our good.

In God's economy, trials and tribulations become stepping-stones to exaltation, turning conventional thinking on its head. Opportunities for personal growth disguised as challenges reveal themselves as blessings and aids in our eternal quest. Today's trials can become tomorrow's testimonies, shaping us in the image of the Master. Conversely, what is generally considered good fortune such as wealth, education, and distinction can become stumbling blocks to individual progression if not channeled in the service of God and our fellow human beings.

A skeptic might respond, "That's easy for you to say. You are not the one born into poverty or one of the six million Jews who lost their lives." This protestation presents a powerful point; namely, none of us knows exactly how well we would respond if confronted with the challenges others endure. We should be humbled by our own fortunate circumstances and feel deep empathy when we see the suffering of others. We can view their situation with genuine compassion that moves us to serve and lighten their load as they struggle through a customized course of instruction in life. In this way, the trials of others can be for our good, too, if "we are willing to mourn with those that mourn, yea, and comfort those that stand in need of comfort" (Mosiah 18:9).

In the Lord's providence, another good can result from adversity. When asked why Abraham had to pass through his unimaginable trial, President Hugh B. Brown responded, "Abraham needed to learn something about Abraham" (Truman G. Madsen, *Joseph Smith the Prophet*, 93). So it is with each of us. When the Lord stated, "We will prove them herewith, to see if they will do all things whatsoever the Lord their God shall command them" (Abraham 3:25), He was not proposing a test to inform Himself, but to reveal to each of us how valiant He already knows us to be.

In the process of coming to know good and evil, we also come to know ourselves, what Lincoln called our "better angels."

Finally, perhaps the sweetest fruit of adversity is that it provides us an opportunity to know our Savior in a very intimate way. In Liberty Jail, the Prophet Joseph was comforted and assured that the Lord was not far removed from his trials and pain. "The Son of Man hath descended below them all" (D&C 122:8). By personal experience, Jesus Christ fully comprehends the depths of our agony. As Alma foretold, "And [Christ] shall go forth, suffering pains and afflictions and temptations of every kind. . . . and he will take upon him their infirmities that his bowels may be filled with mercy according to the flesh, that he may know according to the flesh how to succor his people" (Alma 7:11–12).

Because He suffered so intensely for us, we can feel His love and nobility more perfectly amid our own trials. As one of the Lord's anointed recently taught, "The road to salvation is always through Gethsemane, or else I don't know what discipleship means. . . . Don't miss your chance to make your sacred sacrifice. It is in similitude of the tears the Savior shed" (Jeffrey Holland, singles' conference address).

Because our Lord and Savior Jesus Christ willingly descended below all things so as to comprehend all things we are passing through, we can draw closer to Him in our times of affliction (D&C 88:6). As we contemplate the price He paid to fill His bowels with mercy toward us, our hearts should expand with gratitude for His perfect love and Atonement, which have made all good things possible, even afflictions and trial.

# CHAPTER 7

# PROGRESSION AND PAIN

ON THE DEAN'S DESK AT A PROMINENT U.S. SCHOOL OF MEDICINE sits a stone-chiseled paperweight that reads, "Either way will hurt." This highly skilled medical professional is a gastroenterologist, specializing in abdominal surgery. By the time patients are referred to him, they are typically in excruciating pain and facing unpleasant options: continue to suffer or undergo major surgery. "Either way will hurt."

Such is mortal life. "For it must needs be, that there is an opposition in all things" (2 Nephi 2:11). For most, the way forward will require confronting at least one major obstacle, some significant weakness impeding progression. Yet, this is the great opportunity of mortality—to become more like our Heavenly Father and His Son Jesus Christ. This will not be easy.

Progression is an eternal aspect of God's economy. We improved in the premortal sphere and kept our first estate. We entered this temporal sphere to gain a physical body and accelerate the learning process, and "those who keep their second estate [and go on to exaltation] will have glory added upon their heads for ever and ever" (Abraham 3:26). But first, we face difficult options: confront major obstacles or limit our progression. "Either way will hurt."

A few years ago, a man stood in fast and testimony meeting and introduced himself. "My name is Carl Smith (name changed), and I am an alcoholic." My wife and I knew Carl's family well and were aware of his struggles. Before confronting his demons, Carl had hit bottom, losing nearly everything dear to him. He reached a point where he understood without doubt that "either way will hurt." Courageously, he chose the path of complete sobriety, while openly confessing his permanent addiction to alcohol. This is Carl's cross to bear through mortality.

One particularly daunting challenge for some is same-gender attraction. The long-debated issue of genetic programming vs. individual choice fades to irrelevance with a correct understanding of the Lord's great plan of salvation. The divinely ordained pattern in God's economy consists of a family presided over in righteousness by a man and a woman. In our premortal state, we were nurtured as children of a loving Father and Mother in Heaven, and those who abide the celestial law will reign eternally as heads of an expanding family, worlds without end. In becoming like our Heavenly Parents, a family in this life provides the perfect laboratory for learning through hands-on experience. Family is the fundamental unit of the Lord's Church and of society. Yet, those who struggle with same-gender attraction feel drawn in a different direction.

Many years ago, I read with great interest the interview of a Buddhist lama who had apparently mastered all appetites in his quest for enlightenment. The interviewer asked which of all his desires had been most difficult to subdue. He responded that sexual urges were by far the most challenging, adding that if another appetite had been equally compelling, he doubted if he could have overcome it. While the sex drive is not the same for everyone, there is no dismissing this powerful force in human nature. For one with same-gender attraction to "deny himself and take up his cross and follow [the Savior]" is a major challenge indeed (Matthew 16:24).

We all have plenty of the "natural man" in us that manifests itself in "unnatural" habits and obsessions. Those unnatural habits include the use of illicit and prescription drugs, alcohol, tobacco, and pornography. We might become involved in sexual deviances, excessive eating and drinking, video games, and virtual reality. Some of us participate in compulsive gambling, unrestrained pleasure seeking, and risk-taking, along with dealing with the character flaws of unbridled anger, cynicism, and negativity. We might struggle with debilitating fears and phobias, not to mention hypersensitivity, covetousness, envying, gossiping, backbiting, and other destructive insecurities. For most, major obstacles reveal themselves in adolescence, and those same battles rage on to the end of mortal life. To paraphrase King Benjamin, "Are we not all addicts to our favorite sins?" (See Mosiah 4:19.) No wonder he referred to this aspect of the human condition as "natural."

Confronting such hardships, we face unpleasant options. We can impede personal growth by giving in to the natural man, or we can confront obstacles that keep us from progressing. "Either way will hurt." In moments of intense struggling, it can be revelatory when it dawns on us, "To this end was I born, and for this cause came I into the world" (John 18:37). This may constitute *our* test of Abraham, and "all those who will not endure chastening [even as Abraham], but deny [the Lord], cannot be sanctified" (D&C 101:5). In other words, we simply damn ourselves or come to grips with our personalized test in mortality.

In the Book of Mormon, the Lord points the way forward for those who would follow him. "And if men come unto me I will show unto them their weakness. I give unto men weakness that they may be humble; and my grace is sufficient for all men that humble themselves before me; for if they humble themselves before me, and have faith in me, then will I make weak things become strong unto them" (Ether 12:27). Like recovering addicts, we must humble ourselves and acknowledge our limitations in confronting major obstacles.

We will not prevail until we set aside excuses and self-justifying rationalizations. When we are completely honest in contrasting our behavior to His perfect example, the Lord shows us our weaknesses. He gives us weaknesses that we may be humble, because until we humble ourselves, we will continue to go it alone, relying on our own strength. Genuinely acknowledging the recurring cycle in our lives of remorse, renewed commitment and relapse softens us to accept our need to rely on His higher power. Then, we can access the enabling power of His Atonement in our lives. With faith in

Christ and His grace to make us whole through His suffering, He will "make weak things become strong." Or, as Paul so beautifully expressed it, "I can do all things through Christ which strengtheneth me" (Philippians 4:13).

Even as we courageously acknowledge our frailties, the adversary is adapting his tactics, whispering, "You don't really want to take this challenge on right now. There will be time to repent later." Like the chain smoker who tells himself he can quit smoking anytime . . . after all, he has quit a number of times already . . . so we are tempted to postpone the painful confrontation with our favorite sins. Panicked that we might break free from his enslaving tentacles, Satan offers a temporary reprieve from the inevitable discomfort of true repentance: procrastination. The father of lies tenders one more whopping deceit to obscure the truth: "Either way will hurt." Meanwhile, this wily foe is tightening the cords that bind us to self-destructive habits, knowing that "if we do not improve our time while in this life, then cometh the night of darkness wherein there can be no labor performed" (Alma 34:33–34).

"And thus he whispereth in [our] ears, until he grasps [us] with his awful chains from whence there is no deliverance; and leadeth [us] away carefully down to hell" (2 Nephi 28:21–22). Satan fully understands not only "either way will hurt," but he also knows that the longer he can convince us to languish in sin, "either way will hurt even more." Because of his chains and the destructive consequences of sin, it will never hurt less than it does right now—either way.

While the work of being made perfect in Christ will continue long after our sojourn in mortality, there is something unique and vitally important about this time on earth. The Prophet Joseph taught, "If a person gains more knowledge and intelligence in this life through his diligence and obedience than another, he will have so much the advantage in the world to come" (D&C 130:19). We must choose to confront our major obstacles, and through diligence and obedience learn the lessons we were individually sent here to learn, or we will be greatly disadvantaged in the world to come. Ultimately, "They who are not sanctified through the law of

Christ must inherit another kingdom . . . they shall return again to their own place, to enjoy what they are willing to receive, because they were not willing to enjoy that which they might have received" (D&C 88:21, 32). Either way will hurt, but we get to choose the outcome. In the economy of God, agency is always respected, along with accompanying consequences (2 Nephi 2:26).

# CHAPTER 8

# WOMEN AND THE PRIESTHOOD

T HE STORY OF ABRAHAM'S TEST SHOULD HUMBLE ANYONE WHO
professes a desire for eternal life. Abraham passed his test, a trial
of faith almost too horrific to imagine. Those who would receive
the blessings of Abraham "must needs be chastened and tried, even
as Abraham . . . For all those who will not endure chastening . . .
cannot be sanctified" (D&C 101:4–5).

After waiting faithfully for ninety-nine years, the Lord blessed
Abraham and Sarah with a son through whom promised blessings
of the covenant were to be fulfilled. Some years later, the Lord
commanded Abraham, "Take now thy son, thine only son Isaac,
whom thou lovest, and get thee into the land of Moriah; and offer
him there for a burnt offering" (Genesis 22:2).

Abraham had another son, Ishmael, born of Hagar, but Isaac
was the "only son" of his beloved Sarah, the chosen seed, the one
Abraham loved with all his heart. Unlike the young man who approached the Savior only to go "away sorrowful: for he had great
possessions" (Matthew 19:22), Abraham would have gladly parted
with his wealth rather than offer up Isaac. For Abraham, the trial of
his faith required the one thing he loved more than anything and
everything else.

As if not horrifying enough, modern scripture informs us that
in his youth Abraham had been delivered miraculously from the

hands of murderous priests who threatened to make him an offering to their false gods. (See Abraham 1.) The intense trauma of that experience must have seared Abraham's mind as he pondered the course of action he was now commanded to take.

How did Abraham make sense of the radical contradictions confronting him? Now the heinous acts of false priests were to become his own. Now the long-awaited child of the covenant must meet his fate at his father's hand. How does one find faith to move forward when the mind is screaming, *This cannot be!*?

The Apostle Paul provides great insight into Abraham's thought processes. "By faith Abraham, when he was tried, offered up Isaac: and he that had received the promises offered up his only begotten son, of whom it was said, That in Isaac shall thy seed be called: *Accounting that God was able to raise him up, even from the dead"* (Hebrews 11:17–19; emphasis added).

Reaching the limits of his finite understanding, Abraham moved forward, exercising faith in a few core truths. It was clear that God had commanded Abraham to offer his beloved son. He was certain God had made a sacred covenant to bless his posterity through Isaac. He also knew God's precious promises would be fulfilled, because God is a God of truth with power to do whatever is necessary to keep his word, including "to raise [Isaac] up, even from the dead." And perhaps most important of all, he knew God loved him and desired to bless him. So while the commandment to offer Isaac contradicted every rational impulse, Abraham went forth, relying on the goodness and power of God to keep all His promises.

Sooner or later, we all reach the limits of our understanding of God and His economy. For some, it occurs when the law of tithing requires a sacrifice that appears impossible given meager resources. For others, the frontier is exposed when efforts fail to reconcile aspects of scientific learning with gospel teachings. Tests of faith always involve some degree of uncertainty. "Therefore if ye have faith, ye hope for things which are not seen, *which are true* (Alma 32:21; emphasis added). Faith is only faith when hope is centered on things that are true, a few core eternal realities. But "faith is not to have a perfect knowledge of things" (Alma 32:21).

For one dear family friend, we shall call her Linda, the test came with her first visit to the temple a few years ago. Linda was "horrified" (her word) by what she perceived as a depiction in the endowment that makes her gender "second-class citizens." In our modern culture, confusion regarding the role of women and the priesthood has become a stumbling block for some, a test of faith for otherwise faithful Saints.

Like Abraham, Linda and others who share her concerns would do well to examine their perceptions of Church teachings in the light of a few core truths. The scriptures are clear and unambiguous: "God is no respecter of persons" (Acts 10:34); neither is He "a partial God" (Moroni 8:18; see also D&C 1:35 and 38:16). Women are loved and cherished by our Father in Heaven no less than men. There are no "second-class citizens" in the economy of God.

This is not to suggest that roles of men and women are the same. In "The Family: A Proclamation to the World," Church leaders have stated, "Gender is an essential characteristic of individual premortal, mortal, and eternal identity and purpose." Basic differences between men and women are absolutely essential to individual happiness and to bringing about the plan of salvation. These differences are eternal in nature and deserve to be celebrated as blessings.

While all aspects of relationships between the sexes in God's economy have not been revealed, it is clear that exaltation and eternal life with God require the complement of both a male and a female. The equality of man and woman in the Lord is not one of sameness but rather of mutual interdependence (D&C 131:1–3). "Neither is the man without the woman, neither the woman without the man, in the Lord" (1 Corinthians 11:11; see also D&C 131:1–3).

For example, to my knowledge, the Lord has never seen fit to clarify whether exalted women will hold the priesthood in their own right or share their husband's priesthood throughout eternity, but one absolute certainty is that women will enjoy all the rights, powers, and privileges appertaining to godliness to the same degree as exalted men. In the economy of God, perfect equality and unity prevail. Fittingly, blessings pronounced at the veil of the temple are identical for both genders. Women will be fully satisfied with the justice of God; otherwise, God would cease to be God (Alma 42:13).

Unwittingly, those who insist on emphasizing sameness between the sexes diminish the uniqueness and complementary aspects of each sex. Rather than competing with men largely on terms that favor men, women would be better served to celebrate qualities innate to their own gender. For example, productivity in the work place has increased significantly in recent years because of greater value given to cooperation and collaboration, qualities associated with feminine sensibilities.

Likewise, motherhood is the most sacred and noble of callings, uniquely and integrally linked to women. It deserves to be extolled and honored above all other privileges but is too often minimized by those who instead adopt worldly values and "aspire to the honors of men" (D&C 121:35). In this, they diminish the holiest defining characteristic of the female gender. Admittedly, it is not easy to elevate motherhood to its proper position in a world that places higher value on wealth, distinction, position, and power, but none of these temporal distractions is of enduring worth. Motherhood is.

A great fear of some women is that they will be subordinate to their husbands in eternity. One of the grand illusions in this life is the idea that holding the priesthood implies superior power and position in this and the next life. As cited previously, the Lord taught His disciples, "Ye know that the princes of the Gentiles exercise dominion over them, and they that are great exercise authority upon them. *But it shall not be so among you*: but whosoever will be great among you, let him be your minister; And whosoever will be chief among you, let him be your servant" (Matthew 20:25–27; emphasis added).

In the economy of God, priesthood is the responsibility to lead in righteousness, serving and ministering unto others. It can only be exercised on principles of righteousness (D&C 121:36). "*No* power or influence [none whatsoever] can or ought to be maintained by virtue of the priesthood" (D&C 121:41; emphasis added). Unrighteous dominion frequently exercised in temporal affairs is not the Lord's way and "shall not be so among" those holding His priesthood.

God's power derives from His pure knowledge, intelligence, and perfect attributes (D&C 121:41–42). He speaks, and intelligences respond in obedience out of awe and reverence (Abraham 4). His dominion is established and maintained "without compulsory means," flowing unto Him forever and ever (D&C 121:46; see also 29:36). The Holy Priesthood, after the Order of the Son of God, can only operate upon similar principles (D&C 107:3; 121:36); otherwise, "Amen to the priesthood or the authority of that man" (D&C 121:37).

The most sublime relationship between a man and a woman will only be perpetuated in the highest degree of glory (D&C 131:1–3). In that sphere where the economy of God operates perfectly, there is neither compulsion nor hierarchy beyond our eternal relationship with the Father and the Son. All others are equal. All are godlike. All abide the same celestial law and draw upon the same powers of godliness (D&C 88:21–24). Callings and offices of the priesthood in this life will be done away. The Church with its hierarchical structure will no longer be necessary. All who attain exaltation will be Gods. The order of heaven is family—a perfect unity between a glorified man and an equally glorified woman.

In the classic movie *The Princess Bride,* a scheming Sicilian, Vizzini, is hired to start a war with neighboring Guilden. As events unfold differently than expected, Vizzini expresses disbelief, uttering the same word of exasperation: "Inconceivable!" Finally, one of his companions, Inigo Montoya, observes, "You keep using that word. I do not think it means what you think it means" (Goodreads.com).

Unless private interpretations of scripture and temple ceremonies are consistent with revealed core truths, inferences almost certainly do not mean what one thinks they mean. Core truths provide firm ground for comprehending the word of God, lest we unwittingly "wrest . . . scripture, unto [our] own destruction" (2 Peter 3:16).

Like the servant of Elisha, when eyes are opened to a larger reality, concerns about power, position, and dominance melt away in the economy of God. The divine organization of the Church serves God's purposes in mortality but is not eternal. What will endure for all time is a family order in which man is totally dependent on woman and woman on man—a perfect unity and equality in the image of a perfect loving Heavenly Father and Heavenly Mother but with different roles necessary to bring to pass God's glorious purposes. These are core truths upon which all can exercise unfailing faith, enabling those like Linda to "trust in the Lord with all [their] heart[s]" (Proverbs 3:5) and pass their own individualized test of Abraham.

CHAPTER 9

# FAITH AND POWER

THOUGH NONBELIEVERS WILL CONTEST THE WORD CHOICE, "faith" is the basis upon which this temporal world operates. This fact is evident in both the mundane and the extraordinary. For example, when an individual climbs out of bed in the morning, it is faith that enables him or her to rise. Their first presumption, conscious or otherwise, must be that they are able to rise if they exert themselves. Without this presumption, they would not make the attempt, and because the presumption is correct, they, indeed, stand. This is faith: to "hope for things which are not seen, which are true" (Alma 32:21).

Likewise, faith was manifest when Albert Einstein conceived his theory of general relativity in pursuit of a life-long quest "to know God's thoughts;" when Abraham Lincoln aspired to be the sixteenth president of the United States; and when the patriarch Abraham "offered up his only begotten son, of whom it was said, That in Isaac shall thy seed be called" (Hebrews 11:17–18.) "If men [and women] were duly to consider themselves . . . they would readily discover that it is faith, and faith only, which is the moving cause of all action in them; that without it both mind and body would be in a state of inactivity, and all their exertions would cease, both physical and mental" (Joseph Smith, *Lectures on Faith*, 1).

Faith is also the basis upon which the economy of God operates. For example, the Apostle Paul informs us, "Through

51

faith we understand that the worlds were framed by the word of God" (Hebrews 11:3). God spoke, the elements responded, and "the Gods watched those things which they had ordered until they obeyed" (Abraham 4:15). This same faith-based process will continue to operate through all eternity as numberless new worlds roll forth. Faith is an eternal principle and a key to understanding how the economy of God operates.

At first glance, Paul's assertion that the worlds were framed through faith might seem surprising. After all, God is all-knowing (omniscient) and all-powerful (omnipotent). Why wouldn't knowledge and power be the basis for worlds that have been, are, and will be?

To comprehend God's work of creation, it is helpful to understand the mechanics of that process to the extent they have been revealed. The basic building blocks of all creation are (1) intelligence, and (2) element. Scripture informs us that intelligence and element are coeternal with God. "Intelligence, or the light of truth, was not created or made, neither indeed can be" (D&C 93:29). Similarly, "The elements are eternal" (D&C 93:33; see also *Teachings*, 181).

God organized the basic building blocks of creation into live matter, combining inert element with vibrant intelligence, making matter "alive." In the words of Brigham Young: "There is life in all matter throughout the vast extent of all the eternities; it is in the rocks, the sand, in water, air, the gases, and in short in every description and organization of matter whether it be solid, liquid, or gaseous, particle operating with particle" (*Journal of Discourses*, 3:227). This is consistent with the Lord's description of "The light which is in all things, which giveth life to all things, which is the law by which all things are governed, even the power of God" (D&C 88:13). All around us, we observe live matter "in which dwells all the glory" (*Teachings*, 351) and the intelligences comprising live matter respond to the ever-present influence of their Creator, Jesus Christ.

Scripture and the temple endowment teach that creation proceeded in two phases: first, spiritual, and second, temporal

(D&C 29:31–32; Moses 3:5–7). This occurred as intelligence first combined with more "fine or pure" matter in the spiritual creation (D&C 131:7–8). Later, intelligence-infused spirit matter combined with temporal matter in the temporal creation as God organized living matter into combinations, producing all things we observe in this world from basic elements of science to complex compounds and organisms in all their varieties (Moses 3:7–9, 19).

According to scriptural and temple accounts, the creation was brought about as God spoke, and living matter responded to the commands of its Creator. Infused with intelligence, live matter recognizes and obeys the voice of its Creator, an act of choice or agency (Abraham 4).

As part of the creation, God instituted laws to accomplish His righteous designs, placing intelligences within defined conditions, but maintaining their independence so that "without compulsory means" His dominion "flows unto [Him] forever and ever" (D&C 121:46; see also *Teachings*, 354). "All truth is independent in that sphere in which God has placed it, to act for itself, as all intelligence also; otherwise there is no existence" (D&C 93:30).

When the Creator speaks, intelligences in live matter respond of their own free will and choice. This was true when the earth rolled into existence as well as when the Savior rebuked the storm, calmed the sea, healed the infirmed, changed water to wine, and performed other miracles. In all these instances, intelligences obeyed their Master's voice based on faith in the Lord Jesus Christ and His perfect, Godlike attributes. "And the Gods watched those things which they had ordered until they obeyed" (Abraham 4:18).

Herein lies God's power. Not that He compels obedience, but that other intelligences willingly obey out of awe and reverence for Him, exercising faith that obedience to His commands will bring forth blessings and rejoicing. "The dust of the earth moveth hither and thither, to the dividing asunder, at the command of our great and everlasting God. Yea, behold at his voice do the hills and the mountains tremble and shake" (Helaman 12:8–9). It is this power that upholds planets, solar systems, and galaxies in their course (D&C 88:42–43; Helaman 12:8–17).

It is this power that Lucifer sought when he rebelled, saying, "Give me thine honor, which is [God's] power" (D&C 29:36). Lucifer desired the "honor" of other intelligences, intending to impose his will upon them. In this, he was fatally misguided. He did not understand that "the rights of the priesthood are inseparably connected with the powers of heaven and that the powers of heaven cannot be controlled nor handled only upon the principles of righteousness" (D&C 121:36).

Coercion and compulsion are completely contrary to the principles of righteousness. Intelligences obey, not because they are compelled to do so, but because they trust and honor God. This is the only basis for sustainable and enduring power. "No power or influence *can . . . be maintained* by virtue of the priesthood [or any other authority], only by persuasion, by long-suffering, by gentleness and meekness, and by love unfeigned; by kindness and pure knowledge" (D&C 121:41–42; emphasis added). The only enduring basis for power is faith exercised by lesser intelligences in God and His perfect attributes. "Therefore, if ye have faith ye hope for things which are not seen," believing that obedience to God will bless you, which belief is absolutely correct and true (Alma 32:21).

> God himself, finding he was in the midst of spirits and glory, because he was more intelligent, saw proper to institute laws whereby the rest could have a privilege to advance like himself. The relationship we have with God places us in a situation to advance in knowledge. He has power to institute laws to instruct the weaker intelligences, that they may be exalted with himself, so that they might have one glory upon another and all that knowledge, power, glory, and intelligence, which is requisite in order to save them in the world of spirits. (*Teachings*, 354)

Based on perfect knowledge and wisdom, God instituted laws and defined conditions or parameters within which intelligences operate independently. Based on faith in His perfect attributes of truthfulness, goodness, love, mercy, justice, judgment, and power, intelligences submit to God's instruction, believing "that they may be exalted with himself."

As literal sons and daughters of God, we have the potential to acquire "all that knowledge, power, glory and intelligence" that He has (D&C 84:38). To attain such an exalted status, we must become as He is, perfect in all Godlike attributes so that when we speak, other intelligences willingly obey commands based "upon the principles of righteousness." Then our scepter, a symbol of recognized power, will be "an unchanging scepter of righteousness and truth; and [our] dominion shall be an everlasting dominion, and without compulsory means it will flow unto [us] forever and ever" (D&C 121:46).

Thus we conclude with the Prophet Joseph Smith, "Faith is not only the principle of action, but of power also, in all intelligent beings, whether in heaven or on earth" (*Lectures on Faith*, 3). So it has been, and so it will be, through all eternity. Like all other good things in God's economy, there is no limit or constraint on the amount of honor, power, and glory available to all of God's children through faith in the Lord, Jesus Christ.

# SECTION III
# THE POWER OF LOVE

# CHAPTER 10

# LOVE NEVER FAILETH

SEVERAL YEARS AGO, I WAS ASSIGNED TO HOME TEACH A MAN WHO had lost his faith. As an active member, he had raised his family in the Church, but when we met, he emphatically proclaimed himself an atheist. After several visits, this good man opened his heart and shared his reason for rejecting any notion of a loving God.

A few years earlier, his son had contracted a terminal disease that eventually took his life. That was trying enough, but death was preceded by a protracted period of intense, excruciating pain. As the end approached, this father prayed with faith, asking that his son be permitted one night of comfort before passing. "If God really exists, He would have granted my simple request," this man insisted. "I wasn't asking that my son be spared, but was it too much to ask for one night's comfort? If there were a loving God in heaven, He would have eased my son's suffering for one night so he could slip away peacefully, but it didn't happen."

This man's experience is not unique. Many are disappointed when the divine will does not conform to their conception of a loving God. In her personal journal, even the noble Mother Teresa questioned the existence of a loving Creator who would permit the squalor and deprivation that overwhelmed her in India. Where is divine love amidst such suffering? (David Van Biema, "Mother Teresa's Crisis of Faith").

Yet, the Apostle John declares, "God is love" (1 John 4:8). This is *the* defining attribute that more than any other quality epitomizes God the Father and God the Son in their relationship with the children of men through all eternity, past, present, and future. This love was manifested most perfectly in the meridian of time. "For God so loved the world that He gave his only begotten Son that whosoever believeth in him should not perish, but have everlasting life" (John 3:16). Divine love—often referred to as charity, the pure love of Christ—"never faileth" and "endureth forever" (1 Corinthians 13:8; Moroni 7:47). But God's love is often manifested in ways that contradict our notions of loving expressions.

Serving a mission with my wife in Trinidad, we attended a fast and testimony meeting in a small ward where several Saints rose to share accounts of their trials and tribulations. Toward the end of the meeting, a returned missionary began his testimony by observing, "God is pouring out a lot of love on this ward, 'For whom the Lord loveth, he chasteneth'" (Hebrews 12:6). It reminded me of Tevye's famous line, spoken as he looked toward heaven in *Fiddler on the Roof*, "I know, I know. We are Your chosen people. But, once in a while, can't You choose someone else?" (Wikiquote.org). For most, chastening is not one of our love languages.

As loving parents, we understand it is neither possible nor wise to meet every expectation of how our children desire to experience love. At times, compassion, mercy, patience, and long-suffering must be suspended in the best interest of the child so that discipline and consequences arising from poor decisions can provide enduring lessons. Often our hearts want to say yes, even when we know our "yes" will not bless. In those moments, it takes courage and a nobler sense of love to stand firm and say "no."

If being a parent is, at times, a thankless job, one can only imagine how absolutely hopeless it is to be the heavenly parent to billions of self-willed spirits, all of whom have their own ideas of how godly love should be dispensed. Despite protestations, divine love refuses to take the easy course by acquiescing to shortsighted demands.

A frequently cited account on the Internet provides a powerful analogy from nature to illustrate the higher wisdom of godly love.

> A man found a cocoon of an emperor moth. He took it home so that he could watch the moth come out of the cocoon. On the day a small opening appeared, he sat and watched the moth for several hours as the moth struggled to force the body through that little hole.
>
> Then it seemed to stop making any progress. It appeared as if it had gotten as far as it could and could go no further. It just seemed to be stuck. Then the man, in his kindness, decided to help the moth, so he took a pair of scissors and snipped off the remaining bit of the cocoon. The moth then emerged easily . . .
>
> What the man in his kindness and haste did not understand was that the restricting cocoon and the struggle required for the moth to get through the tiny opening was the way of forcing fluid from the body of the moth into its wings so that it would be ready for flight once it achieved its freedom from the cocoon. Freedom and flight would only come after the struggle. By depriving the moth of a struggle, he deprived the moth of health.

The anonymous writer concludes,

> Sometimes struggles are exactly what we need in our life. If we were to go through our life without any obstacles, we would be crippled." (Fatherduffy.com)

As fallible humans, we sometimes mistake kindness for love while actually impeding progress and growth.

This should ring true especially for members of The Church of Jesus Christ of Latter-day Saints who are aspiring to exaltation. Being remade in the image of Christ requires a painful transformation, much like the monarch moth. Our Heavenly Father has instituted a perfect plan to bring to pass this righteous end, but the radical metamorphosis will not be easy. Even with the workings of Christ's Atonement in our lives, changes will be jarring and jolting at times. As C. S. Lewis famously penned, "You thought you were being made into a decent little cottage: but [God] is building a palace" (C. S. Lewis, *Mere Christianity*, 160). We should not be surprised when the process ends up requiring more significant and painful change than originally anticipated, and yet we often are.

Once complete, we will be thrilled with the result. It's the messy process required to get us there that we are apt to complain about. Too often, we want to be sanctified without sacrifice, to be purified without passing through the refiner's fire. However, in God's wisdom, this world was structured otherwise. "The strongest oak of the forest is not the one that is protected from the storm and hidden from the sun. It's the one that stands in the open where it is compelled to struggle for its existence against the winds and rains and the scorching sun" (Napoleon Hill, Goodreads.com).

In our premortal state when the plan of salvation was announced, scripture informs us that we shouted for joy (Job 38:4–7). Elder Jeffrey R. Holland observed, "Sometimes we wonder what all the shouting was about" (Mid-Singles Conference, 2013). In that grand council, the proposition that we could become like our Father in Heaven through Jesus Christ must have exceeded our wildest dreams. However, premortal jubilation can seem academic and distant in the throes of wrenching growth.

What endowed us with courage and wisdom in that premortal state to embrace the plan of salvation with its inherent challenges and uncertainties? What power sustains us during difficult times in mortality?

It cannot be knowledge alone, because the limits of our understanding are often reached before we have drained the bitter dregs from our relatively small cup. It cannot be our doctrine and belief system alone because the "substance of things hoped for" and the "evidence of things not seen" do not always appear in time to affirm our faith (Hebrews 11:1). What provides the impetus to endure when reason and faith prove inadequate?

As always, we must look to the Great Exemplar for answers: He who suffered "more than man can suffer, except it be unto death (Mosiah 3:7); He who was rejected, reviled, tortured and crucified; He who descended below all things (D&C 88:6). If we can understand what allowed Christ to bear up under His unfathomable load, we may be able to draw from that same source.

In section 19 of the Doctrine and Covenants, the Savior shares that intimate moment when He reached the zenith of His suffering and "would that (He) might not drink the bitter cup, and shrink." He then provides this crucial insight: "Nevertheless, glory be to the Father, and I partook and finished my preparations unto the children of men" (D&C 19:18–19).

"Glory be to the Father!" This was the sustaining power that allowed Jesus Christ to endure "even more than man can suffer, except it be unto death" (Mosiah 3:7). But what does this phrase mean?

Moses used parallel language to record a profound insight given him by the Lord. "This is my work and my glory—to bring to pass the immortality and eternal life of man" (Moses 1:39). The glory of the Father is the immortality and eternal life of His spirit children. In the moment of most exquisite suffering, what sustained the Savior to empty the bitter cup was His love for the Father (glory be to the Father) and His love for His brothers and sisters—you and me—we who are the Father's glory. The thought of being with us in the presence of the Father was more powerful and compelling than the suffering He was required to bear, and so He endured all things. Such is the pure love of Christ, and thus "He partook and finished His preparations unto the children of men."

Moroni informs us that "all things must fail." The strongest self-will cannot persevere. The most regimented discipline will not sustain. The most dogged determination will fall short. Even hope and promise of eternal rewards will not see us through to the end. Charity, and only charity, "never faileth." "The pure love of Christ . . . endureth forever" (Moroni 7:46–47). This was the sustaining power that allowed our Savior to complete His Atonement!

Three times the resurrected Lord asked His chief Apostle, "Simon, son of Jonas, lovest thou me?" (John 21:15–17). He did not ask, "Are you committed, disciplined, and determined?" He did not query, "Are you sufficiently inspired and motivated with promises of eternal glory?" Instead, He sounded out Peter's heart: Do you love me? Because only deep, abiding love "suffereth long . . .

beareth all things, believeth all things, hopeth all things, endureth all things" (Moroni 7:45).

And what does that Christlike love center on? "Thou shalt love the Lord thy God with all thy heart, and with all thy soul, and with all thy mind . . . [and] Thou shalt love thy neighbor as thyself" (Matthew 22:37–38). Love of God and love of fellow beings—all other sources of strength and motivation would have failed to sustain the Savior through the exquisite anguish of Gethsemane, through the physical and mental torture of the trial, and through the cruelty of the cross. And all other sources would have proven insufficient to sustain Peter along the path of discipleship.

One of the defining characteristics of charity is its two-way flow of power. We love the Lord, and we feel His sustaining love for us. The inspiring poem by Emma Lou Thayne, later put to music, beautifully states this truth. "Where can I turn for peace? Where is my solace? Who, who can understand? He only One." (See *Hymns*, no. 129.) Only God's love whispered through the Spirit strengthens and fortifies our love, supplying "substance of things hoped for" and "evidence of things not seen" to see us through all trials (Hebrews 11:1). When the mind reaches the limits of its finite understanding, only God's love endures with "peace . . . which passeth all understanding" (Philippians 4:7).

In these expressions, God's love is deeply personal and intensely intimate. It does not right all the wrongs of this fallen world, nor does it provide definitive answers to all our questions. Yet, it whispers peace to quiet a troubled heart, one heart at a time. As Elijah was taught, "The Lord was not in the wind, and after the wind an earthquake: but the Lord was not in the earthquake: And after the earthquake a fire; but the Lord was not in the fire: and after the fire a still small voice" (1 Kings 19:11–12). Divine love seldom calms the storms, quells the earthquakes, or extinguishes the fires of adversity. Rather, God's love comes with matchless power in a still, small voice that pierces to the core, distilling peace upon the soul, when we are sufficiently humble to hear. "Be still, and know that I am God" (D&C 101:16).

As Elder D. Todd Christofferson recently counseled, "He will sustain you as you work and watch. In His own time and way He will stretch forth his hand to you, saying, 'Here am I'" ("The Power of Covenants").

Tried in the crucible of Liberty Jail, the Prophet Joseph Smith cried out, "O God, where art thou? And where is the pavilion that covereth thy hiding place?" (D&C 121:1). Pleading for divine intervention to "avenge us from our wrongs" (D&C 121:5), the Lord's response came with solace, not justice. "My son, peace be unto thy soul" (D&C 121:7). "He answers privately, Reaching (our) reaching . . . Constant he is and kind, Love without end" (*Hymns*, no. 129). His love sustains us, even when, in His wisdom, relief is forestalled.

God's love was there in the councils of heaven before the creation of this world. It comforts and upholds us amidst mortal pain and trials in His own time and way. In a future day, God's love will exalt us on high to live in His presence eternally with the Son if "we suffer with him, that we may be also glorified together" (Romans 8:17). This is the ever-present, never-failing constant in God's economy.

"What is man, that thou art mindful of him? And the son of man, that thou visitest him?" (Psalm 8:4). God loves each of His sons and daughters with a perfect love, and He is ever mindful of each one, "for he cares for you" (1 Peter 5:7). So it also is with the Son of God. This truth matters most: Their perfect love never faileth.

# CHAPTER 11

# SANCTIFYING LOVE

WHEN FEELING IN NEED OF COMFORT AND CONSOLATION, A favorite scripture is the so-called psalm of Nephi as recorded in the fourth chapter of 2 Nephi. The preceding sixty-plus pages of the Book of Mormon relate events establishing the integrity and nobility of Nephi's character. Perhaps the death of his beloved father and the humbling realization of looming leadership were factors. The scriptures do not provide a definitive reason for the sudden and unexpected baring of Nephi's soul when he cried out, "O wretched man that I am! Yea, my heart sorroweth because of my flesh; my soul grieveth because of mine iniquities. I am encompassed about because of the temptations and sins which do so easily beset me" (2 Nephi 4:17–18).

The Apostle Paul expressed similar feelings of human failing, confessing, "But I am carnal, sold unto sin. For that which I do, I allow not: for what I would, that do I not; but what I hate, that do I. . . . O wretched man that I am!" (Romans 7:14–15, 24).

Measured against the yardstick of our Savior's perfect life, we all fall woefully short. Relapsing in recurrent sin and disappointment, we feel our deficiencies most poignantly. Then, it is comforting to know that truly valiant souls like Nephi and Paul have experienced our remorse and sorrow, while finding strength in the outstretched arms of the Lord to recommit and renew the struggle.

By contrast, the scriptures describe a condition in which the heart undergoes a mighty change producing "no more disposition to do evil, but to do good continually" (Mosiah 5:2; see also 4 Nephi 1:1–18 and Moses 7:18–19, 68–69). In this blessed state, one puts off the natural man, becoming sanctified and holy in the image of Christ. Oh, what a wondrous condition to escape the pull and drag of sin and temptation in this life! What could possibly bring about this mighty change of heart amidst a fallen world? The spirit cries out with hope borne of righteous desire, "O Lord, sanctify my soul."

Unfortunately, we know all too well by experience that will-power and personal resolve by themselves will not bring a permanent change of heart. In fact, there is an inherent danger in rigid self-denial and unbending conformity to law. As memorably illustrated in Victor Hugo's classic novel *Les Miserables*, Inspector Javert's unyielding commitment to justice and rectitude calloused his soul to the cries of merciful compassion and loving goodness. By comparison, the sanctification process softens rather than steels the heart.

At some point, even the most disciplined and strong-willed have to acknowledge that they won't succeed on their own. We are all dependent upon God's grace to change us. The Lord assures us, "My grace is sufficient for all men that humble themselves before me" (Ether 12:27).

Still, grace is not free. "It is by grace that we are saved, *after all we can do*" (2 Nephi 25:23; italics added). We have to do our part. Even Protestant friends, denying good works and attributing all righteousness to the indwelling of the spirit, have to acknowledge relapses and ongoing struggles with temptation and sin. We will not experience a full change of heart without our best efforts combined with the Lord's grace.

So what is our role in the sanctification process? How do we strike the balance between righteous striving and divine grace that can remake us in the image of Christ so we have "no more disposition to do evil, but to do good continually"? In the economy of God, how do we access such transformational power?

The story is told of a young man who approached Socrates and asked him how to acquire wisdom and knowledge. Socrates said, "Follow me," and led him down to the seashore. Once on the shore, Socrates abruptly grabbed the young man and held Him under water until air bubbles surfaced. The young man struggled desperately, and just before he blacked out, Socrates pulled Him up, exclaiming, "When you want wisdom and insight as badly as you desired that breath of air, then you shall have it" (Benjamin P. Hardy, "Quotes That Will Reshape Your Life"). Similarly, Christ-centered discipleship begins with an exceedingly intense desire, yet there is something more.

Many years ago, I had my own Socratic moment of sorts, which provided insight into that "something more." Our young family was vacationing in and around Yosemite National Park. On one of our daily sorties, I persuaded our oldest daughter, Marianne, who was about seven years old at the time, to forge a rapid stream with me. Holding her hand, we ventured into the flow, but in retrospect, I clearly misjudged the force of the onrushing water. Before we had reached mid-stream, Marianne's legs were swept from under her. Positioned upstream from me, her body slammed into my legs, knocking me over. In an instant, I found myself under water on my back still holding onto our daughter, being carried along helplessly by the force of the stream.

My first thought was to make sure Marianne's head was above water to preserve her life and minimize her trauma. My second thought was to get her close enough to a bank so I could push her to safety. I was aware of gnarling debris downstream that might inflict injury if smashed into or, worse, trap me beneath the water, but these impending dangers were considerably less compelling to me than the safety and well-being of our daughter.

Maneuvering as best I could with infrequent gasps of air, I eventually got close enough to the bank to push our daughter to safety. I then turned my attention to the oncoming brush and bramble. Fortunately, I was able to catch hold of a branch, gather my feet beneath me, and make my way to solid ground.

I have reflected on this incident many times, and even now, I am slightly in awe of my reactions. Not that I see in them anything particularly noble or exemplary. I suspect most parents have experienced at least one similar moment when individual self-preservation is completely subordinated to a child's well-being. What is fascinating to me is how instinct completely dominated in the moment. While my conscious thoughts quickly took stock of the situation, my predominant concern was safeguarding our daughter. It was not a deliberate choice or even a rational thought. It was purely instinctual with an absolute, fixed determination that she be protected at all cost.

In the intervening years, this experience has taken on special significance because of its shaping influence on my understanding of the power of love. The Savior taught, "Greater love hath no man than this: that a man lay down his life for his friends" (John 15:13). This type of love is neither rational nor calculating. It is not centered on self. Rather, it is a higher form of love.

As is well known, the Greek language uses several words to express specific aspects or types of love. *Eros,* root of the English word erotic, is physical, passionate love most frequently associated with romantic emotion and sensual desire though not necessarily sexual. It is intensely intimate, directed at the person of one's special affection.

*Philia* love is more general, denoting affectionate regard or friendship. It entails more of a give-and-take relationship with feelings of virtue, loyalty, and goodwill toward others. The eastern U.S. metropolis of Philadelphia takes its name from this word, meaning city of friendship or brotherly love.

A third kind of love, *Agape,* is highly spiritual and sacrificial. It is unconditional and selfless, giving and expecting nothing in return. It is the word used in 1 Corinthians, chapter 13, where Paul expounds on charity, and it corresponds to the pure Christlike love extolled by Moroni (see Moroni 7:47). This is the love referred to above by the Savior: "Greater love hath no man than this: that a man lay down his life for his friends." It is the instinctual love of a parent, willing to make any sacrifice to preserve the well-being of his or her child. It is the perfect love of Jesus Christ, who willing laid down his life for all humankind.

My experience with my daughter has taught me that my love for God and His Son is not yet *Agape*. It is too *Philia* or general—more "good-will" than "thy will." It is not yet unconditional, instinctual, and sacrificial. If it were, I would look upon temptation the same way I discounted danger as I floated down that stream years ago. I would not be oblivious to the attraction of sin, but my attention would be so riveted on doing the will of the Father and His Son that I would have "no more disposition to do evil, but to do good continually."

Reluctantly, I have to acknowledge that I do not yet love the Lord, my God, with all my heart, soul, mind, and strength. As a result, I recognize the need to strengthen my relationship with God until it becomes *Agape*. This relationship is the "something more" necessary to be sanctified, to be instinctually willing to lay down my life of sin for God. Only in the process of enriching this most important relationship will my heart be changed by the transformational power of love.

As recorded in Mosiah, the people of King Benjamin experienced this mighty change of heart as their beloved leader reminded them of God's dealings with all His children. Hearing and embracing eternal truths taught by one with authority brought about a mighty change in the hearts of those present, and they had "no more disposition to do evil, but to do good continually."

Most of us have experienced flashes of this mighty change when we have partaken of the sacrament worthily and participated whole-heartedly in Sabbath worship. Similarly, when sitting in the celestial room of a temple and contemplating the teachings and application of the endowment, our hearts are changed for a time. Likewise, searching the scriptures daily combined with earnest prayer and deep pondering can produce a powerful effect on our disposition toward doing good or evil. Wrapped in the Spirit that accompanies meaningful worship, we feel its sanctifying effects in our lives.

The Book of Mormon does not indicate just how long this mighty change of heart continued among the people of King Benjamin. It records that they entered into a sacred covenant with the Lord, but only a few chapters later, they appear to have returned to contentions, fighting, and apostasy. Accordingly, Alma queried his listeners, "If ye have experienced a change of heart . . . and felt to sing the song of redeeming love, I would ask, can ye feel so now?" (Alma 5:26).

King Benjamin anticipated this all-too-human tendency to fall away from grace. Throughout his inspired discourse, he implored his people to *remember* the goodness of God in their lives, ending with these words: "And now, O man, *remember*, and perish not." (Mosiah 4:30; italics added. See also Mosiah 2:41 and 4:11.)

*Remember* may be the most important word in all scripture, after the name and descriptors of Deity. It is central to the sacred covenants we renew each Sunday, explicitly in both sacramental prayers: "that (we) do always remember him" (Moroni 5:2; see also Moroni 4:3). It is vital in the process of changing hearts.

The ability of righteous memories to transform our dispositions is illustrated in an account recently shared by the brother of an exemplary Latter-day Saint, a former bishop and mission president. Driving home from work one day, this good man's heart was overwhelmed with negative feelings toward his wife. Instinctively, he pulled his car to a shoulder of the freeway and began praying earnestly to expunge these feelings from his heart. Concentrating his full attention on the many instances when his beloved wife had demonstrated thoughtful kindness and Christlike service to Him and their family, he was able to quickly dispel dark, destructive thoughts and feel deep appreciation for his eternal companion. Remembering the goodness of God and those most precious to us softens our hearts and transforms our dispositions.

In the economy of God, the Lord does not ask us to remember past sins, beating ourselves up with our failings and shortcomings. Rather, He invites us to remember His goodness and love manifest through all time. "Remember how merciful the Lord hath been unto the children of men . . . and ponder it in your hearts" (Moroni 10:3). It is then that transformational power flows into our lives.

The beginning of sanctification is not unfeeling obedience. Rather, it begins with remembering a reality that has always been, is now, and will always be: God's love, the only power that can truly change us. It was so easily accessed in the premortal state, and it will fill our hearts throughout future eons. But in this constrained existence, we must remind ourselves often: "We love him, because he first loved us" (1 John 4:19). When we forget that truth, we separate ourselves from the power to resist temptation and conquer sin. Conversely, when we feel gratitude and thanksgiving, filling our minds continually with recollections of His generous goodness and gentle mercy, we feel the Holy Spirit enfold us. Then we long to please God more than ourselves, and we are transformed through the softening, sanctifying power of love.

O Remember! Remember!

CHAPTER 12

# THE MEANING OF CHRISTMAS

IT HAS BEEN CORRECTLY OBSERVED, "WE CELEBRATE CHRISTMAS because there was Easter."

Still, events surrounding Christ's entry into mortality have great significance in their own right. It is one of the reasons we never tire of hearing, relating, and re-enacting sacred happenings that took place on that night of nights when hope entered this constrained and fallen world.

The scriptures contain several accounts of Christ's birth into mortality. Both Matthew and Luke provide complementary narratives of overlapping events as they transpired in the old world. In the Book of Mormon, 3 Nephi relates glorious manifestations on the American continent attending the birth of Christ. Also, prophetic visions of Isaiah and Enoch are recorded in the Old Testament and The Pearl of Great Price, respectively, foretelling the advent of Christ's birth.

My personal favorite of all scriptural accounts is found in 1 Nephi, chapter 11, at the very beginning of Nephi's glorious vision. As recorded, the young prophet was "caught away" into an exceedingly high mountain and spoke with the Spirit of God "as a man speaketh" (1 Nephi 11:1, 11). Having beheld a tree exceedingly white and beautiful, Nephi sought to understand the meaning of the tree. In response, the Spirit showed Him a virgin, the mother of Jesus, "exceedingly fair and white" (v. 13). The Spirit then asked this profound question of Nephi: "Knowest thou the condescension of God?" (v. 16).

Condescension means to come down to the level of another. Admitting that he did not fully comprehend the connection between the tree and God's condescension, Nephi responded, "I know that he [God] loveth his children; nevertheless, I do not know the meaning of all things" (1 Nephi 11:17). The angel then explained, "Behold, the virgin whom thou seest is the mother of the Son of God, after the manner of the flesh" (v. 18). Then Nephi was shown "the virgin again, bearing a child in her arms" (v. 20). As a result of witnessing Christ's entry into mortality, Nephi comprehended both the meaning of Christmas as well as the significance of the tree he had beheld. Like Nephi, we will be blessed by pondering the Spirit's question: "Knowest thou the condescension of God?" We can better appreciate that while marvelous events unfolded on earth with the birth of Christ, another set of dynamics was taking place in eternal realms, in the larger reality of God's economy.

Let us explore the condescension of God, first the Son. We know from scripture and inspired statements of prophets that Jesus Christ was Jehovah, the God of the Old Testament. Before entering mortality, Jesus Christ (Jehovah) was the Creator of vast numbers of worlds, including this one. Now imagine, if possible, a God, the Creator of heaven and earth, willingly condescending to step down from His throne on high and entering this life as a helpless infant in the most humble of circumstances. In the words of one of our hymns: "The King of Kings left worlds of light, Became the meek and lowly one" ("Thy Will, O Lord, Be Done," *Hymns*, no. 188).

In tender moments in the stable, we are left to wonder if Mary and Joseph understood this small, helpless infant framed the world and all that is in it. Is it possible that when she held her baby close and caressed him, Mary recognized she was kissing the cheek of her maker, the great I Am? When he cried out for warmth and nourishment, did His mortal mother and paternal guardian recognize the voice of Him who had commanded the elements in the creation until they obeyed and would soon do the same in rebuking the storm, calming the seas, and healing the sick, the blind, and the lame? Did they understand the condescension of God?

With perfect foreknowledge, the great Jehovah stepped down from His throne on high and came into this world to suffer all manner of temptation, pain, grief, and rejection. In the garden of Gethsemane, He bled from every pore and suffered more than one can endure without lapsing into unconsciousness, which was followed by His death. On the cross, He willingly relinquished His life, dying a most public and ignominious demise between two thieves.

The scriptures tell us that He did all this for you and me to satisfy the demands of justice, atoning for our sins "that he may know according to the flesh how to succor his people according to their infirmities" (Alma 7:11–12). In His unfathomable suffering, He descended below all things to comprehend all things personally (see D&C 88:6). Accordingly, there is nothing we can experience that he has not experienced more poignantly. In the words of a recently penned Christmas song: "Mary, did you know . . . the child that you delivered will soon deliver you?" (Mark Lowry, "Mary Did You Know"). Knowest thou the condescension of God the Son?

Turning to the Father, I have tried to grasp what it would be like to send my firstborn to suffer, bleed, and die for others. My closest personal experience I can relate this to is sending our children on missions for the Church. As a returned missionary myself, I understood challenges awaiting them, as well as joys and glory they would find in serving the Lord. As I hugged my children before their departure, I wept to think I would not be around to comfort them and deflect a portion of their trials and pains. Though I knew it was best for them, and for those they would serve, I could not contain my emotions. My sense of temporary loss and my inability to spare them the full reality of a mission experience was overwhelming.

I think my emotional response must seem insignificant in comparison to that endured by God the Father. An all-knowing, all-loving Father sent His firstborn to face the realities of His Atonement, fully aware of how the Son of man would suffer and call out: "My God, my God, why hast thou forsaken me?" (Mark 15:34).

I have tried to imagine the tender scene as the Father hugged His Son prior to sending Him into mortality. Did He remind Him that all creation depended on His faithfulness?

Or did He simply weep, His heart broken that salvation for all His children required such exquisite suffering by this one Beloved Son? Did the Son respond with reassurances that His entire premortal existence had prepared Him for His earthly mission? Or did He simply promise His Father that He would return with honor? We do not know exactly what took place between the Father and Son on that occasion, but I feel certain it was "exquisitely" difficult to let His Son depart. The Father, who wept before Enoch while viewing the ungodly acts of the residue of His children, must have felt His heart break as He sent His Son into the world to reconcile the rest of us to Him through His beloved Son's Atonement and righteousness. Knowest thou the condescension of God the Father?

With quickened understanding, witnessing the birth of Christ provided answers to Nephi's query to know the interpretation of the tree. It also taught Him the true meaning of Christmas. The angel then asked, "Knowest thou the meaning of the tree which thy father saw?" Nephi replied, "Yea, it is the love of God, which sheddeth itself abroad in the hearts of the children of men; wherefore it is the most desirable above all things." Nephi came to comprehend the extent of God's love for His children by witnessing the birth of Jesus Christ. In this, he understood the depth of love that motivated the condescension of God.

We all have a universal longing to feel loved now and through eternity. As Nephi realized, Christmas reassures us of God's love through the condescension of the Father and the Son. The words of another Christmas song capture this dawning awareness: "Did you know, did you know, it was God's own Son, the salvation of the world begun? Did you know it was love that was sent from above to the earth?" (Natalie Sleeth, "Were You There on That Christmas Night?").

With insight born of the Spirit, we can feel God's love in our hearts more fully each Christmas. We can marvel at the condescension of God, both the Father and the Son, in their acts of pure love that provide us the only way to return to God, who is our home. They love us with a perfect love now and through eternity.

It is no wonder we never tire of hearing, relating, and re-enacting the events that took place on that night of nights. God's love for His children is the ultimate reality that defines God's economy, freeing us from the stifling constraints and disabling despair of mortality.

# Section IV
# The Infinite Atonement

# CHAPTER 13

# TIME AND ETERNITY

AMONG THOSE WHO STUDY ANIMALS, IT IS CONJECTURED THAT A fish is oblivious to water. Especially for deep-sea species, a fish's life transpires immersed in abundant liquid. The law of opposites states, "Wherefore, if it should be one body it must needs remain as dead" (2 Nephi 2:11). A fish that only experiences "one body" and is always immersed in water perceives no water at all. To the fish, water "must needs remain as dead," as if it does not exist.

In mortality, the human counterpart to this phenomenon is time. Not that humankind is oblivious to time. It is quite the opposite. So immersed in the incessant flow of one moment to the next, the human mind simply cannot conceive existence outside of time. Our whole life experience is perceived through the lens of linear time: past, present, and future. As the beloved hymn teaches, "Time flies on wings of lightning; we cannot call it back. It comes, then passes forward along its onward track" ("Improve the Shining Moments," *Hymns*, no. 226). It is part of the human experience in which God "hath given a law unto all things, by which they move in their times and their season" (D&C 88:42). Linear time appears as an immutable law in this mortal state.

But this was not and will not always be so. Alma informs us, "Time only is measured unto men" (Alma 40:8). Scripture repeatedly proclaims that when the millennium is ushered in, "there shall be time no more" (D&C 88:110; 84:100 and Revelation 10:6) In

God's economy, if time exists at all, it is radically different, so much that "time will be no more" as we know it now.

Until that day, God will communicate to His children in terms they understand (2 Nephi 31:3), which of necessity will reference time. Indeed, some scriptures refer to time when describing eternal things. For example, the Lord's definition of truth is expressed in terms that speak to man's sense of time: "knowledge of things as they are [present], and as they were [past], and as they are to come [future]" (D&C 93:24). This is not because time, as we know it, is eternal, but because we simply cannot make sense of eternal things in our present state without reference to linear time.[1]

One difference made apparent in scripture is that the flow of time in the sphere in which God operates is not linear. Rather, "all things are present" before His eyes (D&C 38:2; see also Moses 1:6), And "all things . . . are manifest, past, present and future . . . continually" (D&C 130:7). This radical time warp, what Elder Neal A. Maxwell and some philosophers have referred to as "an eternal now," allows God to know all things (*Plain and Precious Things*, 57; see also 2 Nephi 2:24; 9:20; 27:27; Mormon 8:17; and Moroni 7:22). Accordingly, He comprehends the end from the beginning (Abraham 2:8). He "knows all things to come" and makes provision for man's weaknesses in preparing a way to accomplish His purposes.

For example, the Lord provided a second set of records, the small plates of Nephi, knowing in advance that fifteen hundred years later, Martin Harris would foolishly lose 116 pages of translation taken from the large plates (Words of Mormon 1:7). Similarly, God foreordains leaders according to His foreknowledge of their greatness and nobility (Abraham 3:23–25; Alma 13:3, 7).

In His work, God does not conjecture, project, or speculate. Rather, He "knows" because all things past, present, and future are continually before His eyes. As Elder Maxwell taught, "His is not simply a predicting based on the past. In ways which are not clear to us, [God] actually sees, rather than foresees the future" (Maxwell, "A More Determined Discipleship"). So while "time and space are real, not illusions . . . God created them both and is not bound by either" (*Plain and Precious Things*, 57).

We also learn in scripture that it is possible for man to experience this radically altered state of time. For example, the Brother of Jared beheld, "all the inhabitants of the earth which had been [past], and also all that would be [future] . . . for he knew the Lord could show Him all things" (Ether 3:25—26). Also, "Moses beheld the world and the ends thereof [future], and all the children of men which are [present], and which were created [past]" (Moses 1:8). Likewise, Enoch was shown "all things, even unto the end of the world" (Moses 7:67), as was John the Revelator (Revelation 1:19), Isaiah, Ezekiel, Daniel, Zechariah, and others favored to behold visions of eternity. In a transfigured state, individuals have experienced eternity where time, as we know it, is no more.

Expanding our concept of "eternity" to account for nonlinear time can add new insights to scriptural teachings. For example, the Apostle Peter taught, "But, beloved, be not ignorant of this one thing, that one day is with the Lord as a thousand years, and a thousand years as one day" (2 Peter 3:8; see also Psalm 90:4 and Abraham 3:4). Many have supposed this to be a literal equation: one day with God equals one thousand years with man.

However, "one thousand" also symbolically signifies "a 'multitude' or that which is 'incalculable'" (Gaskill, *The Lost Language of Symbolism*, 139). One day with the Lord may also equate to the whole of eternity, "that which is incalculable." This interpretation seems more consistent with Alma's declaration, "All is as one day with God" (Alma 40:8). Perhaps this time relationship is implied when the Lord proclaimed to Moses, "I am without beginning of days or end of years. Is not this endless?" (Moses 1:3). In linear time, we simply cannot conceive of eternity "without beginning of days or end of years," but when time is one continual present, there are no days or years and no beginning or end.

As referenced in chapter 7, when considering what one like unto God pronounced, "We will prove them herewith, to see if they will do all things whatsoever the Lord their God shall command them" (Abraham 3:25), the logical question is, "Prove to whom?" Since God "knoweth all things, and there is not anything save he knows it" (2 Nephi 9:20), we assuredly are not proving ourselves to God, for He already knows the valiancy of each of His children and their ultimate attainment. The one to whom we are proving ourselves is our self. On Judgment Day, there will be no cry of injustice, no charge of arbitrary capriciousness. While all will be wholly dependent on the righteousness of Jesus Christ, each will know by experience if he or she has passed his or her individualized test. We are proving ourselves to ourselves in linear time, so we can discover what God already knows: our personal valiancy through all eternity.

Additional implications of nonlinear time can change perceptions of our relationship with Christ. In linear time, we routinely speak of our Savior's Atonement in the past. Christ's suffering is finished; our souls have been ransomed with all humankind. In linear time, the past can affect the present and the future, but not the other way around. Today's choices will not alter the past because the past is past. More specifically, grievous sin committed today does not add to the price previously paid by the Savior in Gethsemane and on the cross, because the Atonement was completed almost two thousand years ago in linear time.

However, two additional factors come into play, which changes our perspective. First, while Christ has borne our sorrows based on foreknowledge of our choices, we do not know, in advance, what choices we will make. This is crucial in preserving our moral agency. It also means that we approach each choice with complete freedom to choose virtue or sin and the accompanying consequences.

The reason this is so significant in our relationship with Christ is tied into the second factor: in nonlinear time, the choice we make today figures into the price our Savior paid in Gethsemane and on Golgotha. The present affects the past. The Atonement required a foreknowledge of our choices so the price of our sins could be paid, but this implies our choices today either added to or remitted an increment of suffering borne by the Lord in the past. In other words, when we choose sin, we choose to add to the suffering of our best friend, and when we choose obedience, we reduce His burden, though the price was paid in full almost two thousand years ago.

Lyrics to the hymn "This Is the Christ" speak of this reality and invite us to ponder, "How many drops of blood were spilled for me?" (James E. Faust, Jan Pinborough, and Michael F. Moody, as sung by the Mormon Tabernacle Choir).

Past sins are past and cannot be called back. We can only rely on the Atonement to wash us clean of past misdeeds. However, present and future choices are another matter, and we can indeed affect "how many more drops of blood were spilled for us" as a result of choices we have yet to make.

This makes the Atonement of Jesus Christ profoundly personal. Our choices today affected the suffering of our Lord in Gethsemane and on the cross. It is within our power to add to or reduce the load Christ bore for us. It can't get much more personal than that.

Perhaps this adds a new layer of meaning to His teaching, "If you love me, keep my commandments" (John 14:15). If you love me, don't add to my suffering borne for you. Our relationship with Christ is based purely on love. Do we love the Savior enough to cease and desist from activities that contributed to His suffering, or do we love our sins more than we love him?

The pain borne by the Savior was very real, "which suffering caused myself, God, the greatest of all, to tremble because of pain, and to bleed at every pore, and to suffer both body and spirit—and would that I might not drink the bitter cup, and shrink" (D&C 19:18). We confront choices each day that reveal what we love more—wealth, position, pleasure and the natural man, or our Lord Jesus Christ. How many more drops of blood were spilled for you? For me?

Each Sunday as we partake of the sacrament, we covenant to "always remember him" (D&C 20:77). Knowing we can affect the suffering He bore for us should make it significantly easier to always remember Him and desire with all our hearts to add no more to His ordeal. Our hearts should break when we grasp our culpability for inflicting pain on our Lord, when it lies within our power to mitigate it. If we had been privileged to be in the garden or at the foot of the cross to witness His agony, surely we would have longed with every feeling of our souls to relieve His pain. Each day, we should desire with our whole beings to forsake our sins and contribute no more to His suffering, though it is finished.

This relationship is counter-intuitive to our finite minds, because, in our experience, time always flows in one direction. Only in the realm of nonlinear time can the present and future affect the past. The reality of present choices affecting the past is difficult to grasp, immersed as we are in the flow of linear time. Yet, water is there all the time for the fish, perceived or not, and our intimate relationship with Christ is an ever-present reality we cannot escape.

---

## NOTE

1. When asked, "Is not the reckoning of God's time, angel's time, prophet's time, and man's time, according to the planet on which they reside?" the Prophet Joseph Smith answered, "Yes" (D&C 130:4–5). It is interesting to note that the Prophet's answer did not reject the notion of "God's time" outright. We are left to wonder if time only exists in this mortal sphere and the prophet's reply was adapted to human understanding, or if God's time is so radically different from man's, perhaps in another dimension of time, so that time, as we know it, will be no more.

# CHAPTER 14

# THE ATONEMENT OF CHRIST

THE CONSUMMATE TRUTH IN TIME AND ALL ETERNITY IS THE infinite Atonement wrought by the Lord, Jesus Christ. With humility, we must acknowledge that despite additional light and knowledge from modern scripture and latter-day prophets, "It is impossible for us to fully understand how [Jesus Christ] suffered for all of our sin" (*Gospel Principles*, 60). Though we lack a perfect understanding of the laws and conditions that made the infinite Atonement possible, still we are able to glimpse, in part, the workings of the economy of God in which the ultimate victory was attained.

It was not enough that Jehovah, God, Creator of heaven and earth, condescended to enter this world as a helpless infant. Nor was it enough that this lone man had lived a perfect life, one in complete harmony with the spirit. Even the reality that He had gone about "doing good," healing the sick, giving sight to the blind, causing the lame to walk, and raising the dead was insufficient. The winds and the waves had obeyed His commands. He had organized His Church, ordained men with priesthood power, and taught the doctrines of salvation. All of this was necessary to qualify Him to be "the lamb slain from the foundation of the world" (Revelation 13:8), but insufficient to redeem humankind. He must now finish the work He was sent to do. This time the knife would not be stayed. He must "descend below all things that he might comprehend all things" (D&C 88:6) and "know according to the flesh how to succor his people" (Alma 7:12).

As He entered the garden, Jesus remarked how His spirit was "very heavy," "exceeding sorrowful unto death" (Mark 14:33). He surely knew, "To this end came I into the world, and for this cause was I born" (John 18:37). Yet, as the poignant reality of being "wounded for our transgressions" (Isaiah 53:5) began to weigh down upon him, He marveled at the pain.

Artists generally depict a dignified Jesus kneeling and praying in the garden, but scripture suggests a different scene. Matthew informs us that Jesus "fell on his face" (Matthew 26:39). Mark tells us He "fell on the ground" (Mark 14:35) and was "sore amazed" (Mark 14:33), not fully anticipating the extent of His agony. Luke provides more detail. As the Lord suffered, "There appeared an angel from heaven, strengthening him. And being in an agony, He prayed more earnestly: and His sweat was as it were great drops of blood falling down to the ground" (Luke 22:43–44). King Benjamin informs us it was "even more than man can suffer, except it be unto death; for behold blood cometh from every pore, so great shall be his anguish for the wickedness and the abominations of his people" (Mosiah 3:7).

When confronted with intense pain, our bodies are constructed to first lapse into a state of unconsciousness, known as syncope. Should the pain continue with sufficient poignancy, death takes hold, the spirit being wrenched from its mortal frame. No such relief would rescue our Savior. Jesus Christ had received from His Father "power to lay [down his life] and power to take it up again" (John 10:18). No combination of individual acts or circumstances could cause Him to lose consciousness or pass through the portal of death until He willed it so. The infinite Atonement would require super-human godly powers as well as the Savior's full concentration to "bear our grief and carry our sorrows" (Isaiah 53:4). Only a God, one endowed with power over death, could endure the full agony of Gethsemane and Calvary. To be an infinite Atonement, a God must suffer, bleed, and die.

"The chastisement of our transgressions" (Isaiah 53:5) which He bore cannot be grasped by the finite mind, "which suffering caused . . . even God, . . . to tremble because of pain, and to bleed from every pore, and to suffer both body and spirit—and would that [He] might not drink the bitter cup and shrink" (D&C 19:18). Speaking of this pain and suffering the Lord informs us, "how sore you know not, how exquisite you know not, how hard to bear you know not" (D&C 19:16). We simply cannot comprehend the price He paid for our sins. In our constrained world, even pain and suffering have defined limits of what can be experienced by mortals, but the agony of our Lord far exceeded those bounds. Such was the price of an infinite Atonement paid by the Creator of heaven and earth, a price beyond human experience and comprehension.

It is worth noting that the Savior's prayer in the garden, as recorded in scripture, was always the same throughout that night. Why the same prayer? "Abba, Father, all things are possible unto thee; take away this cup from me: nevertheless, not what I will, but what thou wilt" (Mark 14:36). In that moment of raw agony, there was nothing more to be said. Crying "Abba," an intimate term perhaps equivalent to "daddy," the Son pled with His Father. If it be possible, let there be another way to pay for the sins of the world. This pain is so amazing, so astonishing, so exquisitely intense. Please show me another way through this. Nevertheless, not my will, but thine be done. In God's economy, there simply was no other way to ransom the rest of us.

In this moment of infinite suffering and anguish, the Lord prayed more earnestly to subordinate His will to the Father's. For all mankind, there is no more perfect lesson in the life of our Savior than this one

As Jesus rose for a third time from the dirt floor of Gethsemane, He must have been spent, both physically and mentally, having passed a sleepless night in unfathomable pain. What He encountered in Gethsemane was borne in quiet isolation, but what lay ahead would play out on a most public stage. He must descend below all things "that his bowels may be filled with mercy, according to the flesh" (Alma 7:12).

First, He was betrayed by one of His closest associates. It could have been anyone. After all, He taught in public theaters every day, but the fact that it was one of His own must have cut more deeply. For anyone who has been betrayed by a spouse or trusted friend, Jesus "knows according to the flesh how to succor his people."

Then, the Savior was abandoned by the rest of His disciples and denied three times by His chief Apostle. For anyone who has been victimized by the cowardice of others, Jesus "knows according to the flesh how to succor his people."

He was taken and tried in a series of illegal trials, first before Caiaphas, next Pilate, then Herod, and finally back to Pilate. The innocent one was judged by guilty, unprincipled men. For anyone who has been wrongly accused and unjustly judged by another, Jesus "knows according to the flesh how to succor his people."

He was condemned to die by Pilate, though this magistrate found no fault in him. However, to satisfy the passions of an irrational mob, Pilate pronounced Jesus deserving of crucifixion. For anyone who has been unfairly condemned or made the pawn in political wrangling, Jesus "knows according to the flesh how to succor his people."

He was subjected to the vilest of insults, epitaphs, verbal assaults, and venomous hatred. For anyone who has felt the sting of discrimination and irrational rejection, Jesus "knows according to the flesh how to succor his people."

He was mocked, humiliated, stripped of His clothing, spat upon, assaulted, and abased. A purple robe was draped on His shoulders and a crown of thorns placed on His head to ridicule and make public display of the so-called King of the Jews. For anyone who has felt marginalized, mocked, and made the brunt of public scorn for the entertainment of others, Jesus "knows according to the flesh how to succor his people."

He was strapped to a column and scourged with a whip. Bits of bone and jagged glass tore into His skin and dug out whole chunks of flesh. Forty lashes were enough to kill weaker men, but not the Savior who endured the torturous blows only to be mocked, tormented, and reviled again. As Isaiah foretold, "He was wounded for our transgressions, he was bruised for our iniquities . . . with his stripes we are healed" (Isaiah 53:5). For anyone who has endured both physical and mental abuse and torture, Jesus "knows according to the flesh how to succor his people."

He was forced to carry the instrument of His own death, but His physical strength reached its limits. He stumbled and fell repeatedly until another was compelled to assist Him on His path to Golgotha. For anyone who has reached the limits of his or her physical or emotional strength, Jesus "knows according to the flesh how to succor his people."

He was branded a criminal, a menace to society, and made a public display of what becomes of those not conforming to societal dictates. Condemned to hang between two justly convicted thieves, can there be any lower status assigned to man? For anyone who has been demeaned or made to feel inferior in a status-conscious society, Jesus "knows according to the flesh how to succor his people."

He was nailed to a cross, stripped of His clothing, and made an object of scorn as others wagged their heads and taunted Him to come down. Yet in these moments of personal rejection, His thoughts turned to His mother, asking His beloved disciple to care for her as if for His own. "Take my mother home." It was too much to see the sadness in her face and the anguish she felt for one she loved so dearly. For anyone who has disappointed a loved one or fallen short of expectations, Jesus "knows according to the flesh how to succor his people."

In agony, He cried out, "My God, my God, why hast thou forsaken me?" (Matthew 27:46; see also Mark 15:34). In Jewish culture of that day, citing the opening phrase of a passage of scripture was to call attention to the entirety of its verses. His cry, "My God, my God, why hast thou forsaken me," is the opening verse of the twenty-second Psalm, a messianic psalm. His cry constitutes a final declaration to the world of His messiahship, as if to say, I am He spoken of in the psalm.

It was also the anguished expression of one left desperately alone as the spirit withdrew completely, the cumulative consequences of all human sins poured out without measure upon the sinless one.

For everyone who has felt the spirit withdraw "even in the least degree" (D&C 19:20) because of his own sins, Jesus "knows according to the flesh how to succor his people."

Totally exhausted, at the weakest, most vulnerable point of His entire life, the Savior of the world was abandoned to descend into the very jaws of hell alone where Satan and his minions would make one last, feverish attempt to break him. At any moment, He could have descended from the cross; He could have proven all His detractors wrong; He could have ended His ordeal. Yet, in this final hour, the Savior endured to the end, absorbing the full fury of hell unleashed upon him. For anyone who has felt totally abandoned and alone in moments of greatest suffering, Jesus "knows according to the flesh how to succor his people."

When the last ounce of bitter gall was drained from the cup of justice, the elements groaned, as if to say, "It is enough." The mortal Messiah announced the same: "It is finished" (John 19:30). Bowing His head, He finally allowed His noble spirit to depart its battered, temporal body. He had completed His condescension below all things. He had finished the work for which He had been sent into the world. He had worked out the infinite Atonement of all humankind.

At this point, it is worth pausing to contemplate a vital question: What could have compelled our Savior, with significant foreknowledge of what lay ahead, to enter into a garden of agony, to endure public humiliation and physical torture, to suffer and die on a cruel cross? I submit to you that only one motivating power could have brought about such a willing sacrifice: Love—love of His Father and love of you and me—the defining quality of His being, for "God is love" (1 John 4:8). Only the pure love of Christ could bring about the Atonement.

It is a worthy and rewarding endeavor to ponder the depths of that love again and again. Just as Christ's suffering exceeds our ability to comprehend the depths of His agony, to that same degree and more, His perfect love exceeds our ability to comprehend His longing to be one with the Father and one with you and me through all eternity.

From a mortal vantage point, the demise of Jesus of Nazareth must have seemed an unqualified defeat. In a constrained reality, nothing seems more definitive than death. That it was preceded by unspeakable suffering and pitiless humiliation served only to make the dissolution more complete. Great sadness filled those who hurriedly prepared the fallen body of Christ for burial and placed Him in a garden tomb as the sun set on that Friday, ushering in the Jewish Sabbath. For His disciples and faithful followers, the remainder of Friday, all day Saturday, and the early hours of Sunday must have been filled with questions, doubts, and puzzlement bordering on despair. Mark tells us the disciples "mourned and wept" (Mark 15:10).

But the empty tomb on Easter morning changed everything. The world would never be the same because of the announcement of angels: "He is not here, for he is risen" (Matthew 28:6). At first, it came as a thunderbolt. This was too good to be true. How could ultimate victory emerge from total defeat? Even after He appeared to the eleven, inviting them to feel the wounds in His hands and feet, Luke tells us that "they . . . believed not for joy" (Luke 24:41). Nothing in the constrained reality of this world could prepare them for the consummate triumph of His Resurrection over death and our redemption from sin.

The reality of the Lord's infinite Atonement should produce a similar joy and awe in each of us. Jesus Christ has burst the bands of death and hell, flinging open the door of salvation to all. His victory over all temporal power is complete, and His arms are outstretched to each of us.

Through His Atonement, repentance from our sins is possible, and repent we must, for this was His message from the beginning of His ministry to the very end, "that repentance and remission of sins should be preached in my name among all nations" (Luke 24:47). This is the joy and the obligation of the Atonement and Resurrection of Jesus Christ for His true disciples.

May we access the power of the Atonement every day as we continue in righteous striving to repent of our sins and honor our covenants, walking in our Savior's footsteps and submitting our will to His. May we feel the hope, faith, and optimism ushered into our lives by the rising sun of that Easter morn and the reality of the empty tomb. Like the announcement of the angels, the plan of salvation with all its promises is almost too good to be true. But in the economy of God, an all-loving, all-powerful Heavenly Father has decreed it so, and our Lord and Savior, Jesus Christ, "has purchased us with his own [precious] blood" (Acts 20:28), making all things possible. May our eyes be opened to this larger reality, perceiving the triumphant truth of God's perfect love for each of us.

# CHAPTER 15

# EASTER MORN

IN HIS AUTHORITATIVE BOOK *MOHAMMAD: HIS LIFE BASED ON EARLIEST SOURCES*, British scholar Martin Ling, a convert to Islam, attempts to document many miracles performed as part of Mohammad's legacy. Many of these miracles are strikingly parallel to those in the ministry of Jesus Christ. Like the magicians of Egypt in the days of Moses, others have performed miracles, but not all miracles are equal (see Exodus 7).

In scholarly surveys, historians often rank Mohammad as the most significant or influential person of all time—ahead of Jesus, Moses, Einstein, and other prominent figures. However, one thing these surveys fail to account for is the one thing that makes Jesus Christ more significant than all others combined. Other figures in history have or will die, their bodies left moldering in a grave. Jesus Christ, and Jesus Christ alone, died and then rose from the tomb on the third day, bursting the bands of death and hell for all humankind. This is the miracle of miracles, the bedrock verity in the economy of God that transcends the most daunting constraint of mortality and death and opens the door to the larger reality of eternal life.

The belief systems of all non-Christians, including modern skeptics and secularists, deny the Resurrection of Jesus Christ despite overwhelming scientifically tested historical evidence supporting the reality of this quintessential event (Gary R. Haberman and

Michael R. Licona, *The Case for the Resurrection of Jesus*, 48–77). But what else would one expect? If Jesus rose from the dead, then He is not just a great prophet, as taught in Islam. He is not just another deity, as taught in the Hindu faith. And He is not just a significant historical figure, as taught in secular circles.

As asserted by Elder D. Todd Christofferson in a recent general conference address, if Jesus Christ rose from the dead, then other truths necessarily follow, including,

1. Jesus had to have been a God, even the Only Begotten Son of the Father.
2. Therefore, what He taught is true because God cannot lie.
3. Therefore, He was the Creator of the earth, as He said.
4. Therefore, heaven and hell are real, as He taught.
5. Therefore, there is a world of spirits, which He visited after His death.
6. Therefore, He will come again, as the angels said and "reign personally upon the earth."
7. Therefore, there is a resurrection and a final judgment for all. (See Todd D. Christofferson, "The Resurrection of Jesus Christ.")

And these eternal verities make Easter morn the most significant event in the history of all humankind and Easter Sunday the most significant day of every year.

Yet, even the Christian world seems to celebrate Christmas much more than Easter. For example, our LDS hymnbook has fourteen Christmas hymns, all familiar and beloved, but only three Easter hymns, of which two are well known. Again, in our LDS traditions, we have ward or branch Christmas parties, but no corresponding Easter celebration. Throughout the Christian world, there is no comparison between the lights, displays, parties, gift-giving, and "peace, good will toward men" that occur during the Christmas season relative to the modest observances of Easter.

Why is this when there would be no reason to celebrate Christmas if not for Easter?

There is assuredly no single reason, but a contributing factor may be the relative ease of relating to birth versus rebirth. Each of us enters this world through the birth process, while no living mortal, save one, has passed through the portal of death and returned to earth. Similarly, childbirth is a never-to-be-forgotten event for both mother and eagerly waiting loved ones. By contrast, the physical demise culminating in death appears so dismal and absolute. Personal experiences make it easy to share the rejoicing of angels announcing the long-awaited birth of the Son of God, but we have no point of reference to identify with the wonder of Easter morn when the angels proclaimed, "Why seek ye the living amongst the dead? He is not here; for he is risen" (Luke 24:5). The joy of Christmas is just easier to imagine than the triumph of Easter.

Even in the celebration of Easter, the Christian community seems to connect more with the suffering of Christ than with His breaking the bands of death. A few years ago, Mel Gibson directed and produced a movie entitled *The Passion of Christ*. The first five minutes of the film were spent on scenes in Gethsemane with only brief, indirect mention made of the Resurrection at the end. The other ninety-plus minutes focused on the physical agony and torture endured by Jesus Christ. Likewise, most of the Christian world uses the cross to symbolize their worship of Jesus Christ. Yet, as observed by President Gordon B. Hinckley, "The cross is the symbol of the dying Christ . . . our message [as Latter-day Saints] is a declaration of the living Christ," which is evidenced by the carved figures of the glorified, resurrected Savior adorning many of our temples and visitors' centers (Gordon B. Hinckley, "The Symbol of Christ").

In a similar vein, the Prophet Joseph Smith declared, "The fundamental principles of our religion are the testimony of the Apostles and Prophets, concerning Jesus Christ, that He died, was buried, and rose again the third day, and ascended into heaven; and all other things which pertain to our religion are only appendages to it" (*Teachings of the Prophet Joseph Smith*, 121). It is worth noting that this list of "fundamental principles" does not explicitly include the suffering or passion of Christ. Perhaps it is implied, but it is clear that Christ's suffering only achieved its ultimate efficacy in His triumphant Resurrection. In other Christian expressions, greater emphasis tends to be placed on Christ enduring the cruelty of the cross, because it seems to be easier for all to relate to a suffering Jesus than to a resurrected Christ, even though our anguish cannot compare to His. In this regard, Latter-day Saints are the exception.

In light of our own experiences, it should not be surprising that those who encountered the resurrected Lord two thousand years ago were amazed and astonished beyond belief and more puzzled and confused than convinced. After all, the women who went to the tomb that Easter morn carried embalming materials to complete a proper burial preparation for the lifeless corpse of Jesus. In the furthest reaches of their minds, they were not expecting the news: "He is not here, for he is risen."

Then in a stupefied state, they attempted to explain events to the other disciples who must have been completely confounded. Whatever was said, the words of those initial witnesses were unconvincing. Luke tells us that the women's accounts were dismissed as "idle tales" (Luke 24:11). Even after Peter and John ran to the empty tomb, the disciples could not believe. The Savior's appearance to Mary Magdalene in the garden and His encounter with two disciples on the road to Emmaus did not dispel their doubts. Mark tells us that the disciples continued to "mourn and weep" and "believed not" (Mark 16:11).

Then Jesus appeared in the closed room, and Luke informs us that the initial reaction of His closest associates was one of terror and fear. They could not comprehend that the Lord had actually resurrected from the dead. They imagined that they were seeing a spiritual apparition from the unknown world.

But the Savior spoke reassuringly. He said, "Behold my hands and my feet, that it is I, myself; handle me, and see; for a spirit hath not flesh and bones, as ye see me have" (Luke 24:39). Even after handling the physical body of the resurrected Lord, these perplexed disciples "yet believed not for joy" (Luke 24:41). It was just too good to be true!

Their reaction becomes more understandable if we consider less dramatic moments when unexpected outcomes have left us "believ[ing] not for joy." A couple of examples will illustrate the point.

After laboring for twenty-six hours and pushing for what seemed an eternity, our oldest daughter entered this world screaming indignantly. The doctor and nurses cleaned up our infant girl just a little and then laid her on her mother's chest. The first words out of my dear wife's mouth were, "Look!!! It's a baby!!!" The doctor responded, "What were you expecting?" Though she'd had nine months to prepare for this moment and clearly understood a baby would result, my wife did not anticipate the exhilaration of birth and the miracle of bringing a fully formed infant into the world. It was so much more than she had imagined. She was astonished and amazed beyond belief: she "believed not for joy."

A second example occurred in game one of the 1988 World Series. Trailing 4–2 in the bottom of the ninth inning with two men on base, the Los Angeles Dodgers called on Kirk Gibson to pinch hit. Gibson had injured both legs in separate instances toward the end of the season, and he was too hobbled to play a position. After icing his legs on and off for eight innings in the locker room, he was sent out to face a future Hall-of-Fame pitcher, Dennis Eckersley. Gibson swung at the first pitch and almost fell to the ground. His legs were so weak he could barely rebalance after swinging through the first pitch. His second swing was equally pathetic. With the count at two balls and two strikes, Gibson suddenly remembered the scouting report which indicated Eckersley's strike out pitch was a backdoor slider. Gibson guessed right. Though he had no power in his legs, Gibson somehow managed to send the ball over the right-field fence for a walk-off home run with a flick of the wrist on his one hand holding the bat. Jack Buck, the TV announcer, made the call in these words: "This is gonna be a home run! Unbelievable! A home run for Gibson! And the Dodgers have won the game, 5 to 4; I don't believe what I just saw! I don't believe what

I just saw! Is this really happening? . . . I don't believe what I just saw!" Jack Buck was astounded beyond belief (see YouTube.com).

Perhaps the unexpected outcome in another sporting event can help us understand just how shocking the Resurrection of Jesus Christ was for His disciples. In the 1980 Winter Olympics, a team of amateur hockey players from the United States who had played together for only a few weeks took on a team of veteran stars from the Soviet Union, some of the best players in the world who had played together for several years. The Soviet team had taken home the gold medal for hockey in each of the previous four Winter Olympics. No one really expected this team of amateurs to win. At best they might compete with honor and then graciously accept inevitable defeat. It was a semi-final game. One game and one winner would go on to compete for the gold.

In the locker room before the game, coach Herb Brooks delivered a speech to his players, immortalized in the movie entitled *Miracle on Ice.*

Great moments . . . are born from great opportunity. And that's what you have here tonight, boys. That's what you've earned here tonight. One game. If we played 'em ten times, they might win nine. But not this game, not tonight. Tonight, we skate with them. Tonight, we stay with them . . . and we shut them down because we can! Tonight, WE are the greatest hockey team in the world. You were born to be hockey players, every one of you. And you were meant to be here tonight. This is your time."

One can wonder if Coach Brooks really believed what he was saying, or perhaps he simply mouthed the words a coach would be expected to say to inspire his players in a similar situation.

As the final seconds of the game wound down with the U.S. leading 4–3, the TV announcer, Al Michaels, shouted into his microphone: "Do you believe in miracles?" Then, as the buzzer sounded, he answered emphatically, "YES!!!" (Wikipedia.com).

Now return to that Easter morn. The Resurrection of Jesus Christ was the last thing any of His disciples expected. Just three days before, they had laid their beloved leader in a tomb. He had suffered a most public and humiliating death. Evil had triumphed over virtue in a most crushing and absolute manner. Where His disciples would go from there was uncertain, but death is beyond doubt. No one returns from the dead!

What these disheartened disciples lacked was a Coach Brooks who could help them see the situation for what it was: "Great moments . . . are born from great opportunity." Jesus Christ had earned the right to be in that tomb. Jesus Christ was born to be in that tomb. Jesus Christ, the greatest of all God's spirit children—more intelligent, more powerful, more loving and filled with more life-giving light than all of God's other spirit children combined—was meant to be in that tomb. This was His time, and He would do what no other could.

On that Easter morn, the total defeat of Friday was transformed into the ultimate victory of all time. Jesus Christ burst the bands of death and hell, and the world will never be the same. There is nothing to compare to the unanticipated triumph of the empty tomb.

One last point: The so-called "Miracle on Ice" was only a game. Christ's Resurrection touches every soul who has ever been or who will ever be born into this world. Christ's Resurrection delivered all humankind from the grasp of Satan and the grips of death. Christ's Resurrection is not for just one moment, one day, or for one millennium. Christ's Resurrection is for all time and all eternity!

This event makes everything else in the economy of God possible: "All other things which pertain to our religion are only appendages to it." Do you believe in the miracle of miracles? Yes! Yes! Yes!

May we feel the rush of amazement and the mindboggling astonishment of humble, profound gratitude. May we fall at His feet, overwhelmed by His goodness and greatness. May we believe with joy!

# CHAPTER 16

# THE INFINITE

SEVERAL YEARS AGO, I WAS APPALLED AND STUNNED AS I LISTENED to a Saturday program on National Public Radio in which a young woman described the pain and suffering endured by a younger sibling in the final throes of cancer. Her description of his pain was not what shocked me, although it was a galvanizing account. Rather, at the end of her commentary, she denied the existence of a God who would permit such suffering and then ridiculed the Savior's Atonement, observing that Jesus suffered for a day while her brother's torment dragged on for weeks and months. In effect, she rejected the idea that Christ's agony, borne in a few hours, could compare to her brother's, which was endured over a much longer period of time.

After an initial reaction of revulsion to such a calloused dismissal of divine love, I found myself pondering the question posed by Enos when his sins were swept away. "Lord, how is it done?" (Enos 1:7).

At the core of this woman's impudence lies a calculus not easily ignored. How did the Savior atone for the cumulative woes of humanity in such a concentrated period of time, bearing our sins, afflictions, temptations and sicknesses? (Alma 7:11). The computation is astronomical for the inhabitants of just one earth, but President Russell M. Nelson informs us that "The mercy of the Atonement extends not only to an infinite number of people, but also to an infinite number of worlds created by [Jesus Christ]" ("The Atonement," 35; see also D&C 76:24 and Moses 1:33). Even more so, "Lord, how is it done?"

Book of Mormon authors use one adjective more than any other in referencing Christ's atoning sacrifice: infinite. "Wherefore, it must needs be an *infinite* Atonement . . . there can be nothing which is short of an *infinite* atonement which will suffice for the sins of the world" (Alma 34:10–14; 2 Nephi 9:7; italics added; see also 2 Nephi 25:16). The dictionary defines infinite as "limitless or endless in space, extent or size; impossible to measure or calculate."

It is impossible for the finite mind to grasp infinity, precisely for the reason that infinity is impossible to measure. For example in mathematics, no number is so large that one cannot add to it. Infinity is never reached or attained; therefore, it is impossible to measure or calculate, limitless and endless.

And yet, the Atonement is not infinite in the sense that it is never reached or attained. The Atonement is finished. The Savior pronounced it so. "Jesus knowing that all things were now accomplished . . . said, it is finished: and he bowed his head, and gave up the ghost" (John 19:28–30). Again, in this dispensation, the resurrected Lord has proclaimed, "I [have] accomplished and finished the will of Him whose I am . . ." (D&C 19:2). The Atonement is complete; the victory is won. The price has been paid once and for all. An infinite sacrifice does not require that Christ suffer throughout all eternity.

So in what sense was Christ's suffering in Gethsemane and on Calvary infinite? As discussed in a previous chapter, Luke informs us that "his sweat was as it were great drops of blood falling down to the ground" (Luke 22:44). In modern scripture, the Savior has provided an additional glimpse into His agony: "Which suffering caused myself . . . to bleed at every pore" (D&C 19:18; see also Mosiah 3:7). What kind of anguish would be required to induce bleeding from "every pore"? It is estimated that an adult human body contains around three trillion pores. While three trillion is a large number, it is not infinite. But try to conceive of the crushing weight required to induce blood-filled perspiration to seep from trillions of pores in the Savior's body.

No mortal can begin to imagine such excruciating pain. It is simply beyond our capacity to experience anything approaching this magnitude of agony. Consider an ancient olive press with its massive grinding stones contracting ever tighter with each turn of the vise. Blood mixed with perspiration oozed from every pore of the Savior's body as the cumulative weight of human sin, sickness, and suffering pressed down on the Redeemer of the world: "How sore you know not, how exquisite you know not, yea, how hard to bear you know not" (D&C 19:15). His agony is impossible to measure in human experience, because it exceeded the threshold that humans can bear. We simply have no reference point to begin to imagine. It is infinite because it cannot be comprehended, measured, or calculated.

But this is not all. His ordeal was not confined to mere physical anguish. The Savior suffered both "body and spirit" (D&C 19:18), submitting to the "fierceness of the wrath of Almighty God" (D&C 76:107). On the cross, the Spirit withdrew completely, leaving the Lord completely alone, and He cried out, "My God, my God, why hast thou forsaken me?" (Mark 15:34).

Imagine the darkest depression of the mind when individuals have described wanting to be "rubbed out," their only desire being to cease to exist. In those moments, the Spirit may withdraw, but never completely (D&C 19:20). Jesus Christ descended into the deepest, darkest depths of hell. He descended below all things (D&C 88:6). He descended below all mass murderers and crazed killers, below the vilest pedophiles and the most reprehensible reprobates, and below the most twisted torturers and fiendish sadists.

"The light which is in all things, which giveth life to all things" (D&C 88:13), always flickering with hope even in our darkest hours was completely withdrawn as Christ hung on the cross. Once more, our finite minds have no reference point to fathom a complete absence of the Spirit. Such depths of morose depression and absolute loneliness cannot be experienced by the human mind, because one would will his existence to cease long before such extremities are approached. Only He who is the Light of the World could bear total darkness, suffering in spirit "more than man can suffer" (Mosiah 3:7). His agony of both body and spirit "was infinite beyond any human scale of measurement or mortal comprehension" (Nelson, "The Atonement").

One reason finite minds cannot fathom the depths of our Savior's suffering is that we cannot do the math of an infinite sacrifice. Elder Neal A. Maxwell taught, "The arithmetic of anguish is something we mortals cannot comprehend. We cannot do the sums because we do not have all the numbers" (*All These Things Shall Give Thee Experience*, 37). For example, the word used by the Lord to describe His suffering is "exquisite." "How exquisite, you know not" (D&C 19:15). Numbers and language fail us when attempting to describe the splendor and perfection of Godly agony. Truly, "we know not." Like infinity itself, the human mind cannot grasp it. Only that Jesus Christ reached the unreachable and attained the unattainable.

Because the Atonement entailed super-human suffering, it follows that "It [could] not be a human sacrifice; but it must be an infinite and eternal sacrifice" (Alma 34:10). In this context, one profound meaning of the words "infinite and eternal" is as a surrogate name for "God." Thus the Savior taught, "For Endless is my name. Wherefore, Eternal punishment is God's punishment. Endless punishment is God's punishment" (D&C 19:10–11). Likewise, an "infinite and eternal sacrifice" is God's sacrifice. Alas, a God must die!

No human sacrifice could satisfy the demands of justice. "There can be nothing which is short of an infinite Atonement which will suffice for the sins of the world" (Alma 34:12). An infinite Atonement requires that "God himself atoneth for the sins of the world" (Alma 42:15). As the great Jehovah of the Old Testament, Jesus had attained godhood prior to His coming to earth. As such, He was qualified to offer such an infinite Atonement. "To this end was [He] born, and for this cause came [He] into the world" (John 18:37), having been "foreordained before the foundation of the world" (1 Peter 1:20). Only a God, infinite and eternal, could bring about an infinite Atonement.

Only a God could atone "for the sins of the world" (Alma 42:15), for every individual act of every person who ever has or ever will live on this earth or on innumerable earths of which He is the Creator. Only a God could "be wounded for our transgressions . . . bruised for our iniquities" and heal us "with his stripes" (Isaiah 53:5).

Only a God could endure "pains and afflictions and temptations of every kind," including our "sicknesses" and our "infirmities" (Alma 7:11–12). Only a God could have "borne our griefs and carried our sorrows" (Isaiah 53:4).

Only a God could take "upon Him death that he might loose the bands of death which bind his people" (Alma 7:12). "He who did not need to die himself was willing to be bound by the chains of death so he could break them for all mankind" (Neal A. Maxwell, "Jesus of Nazareth, Savior and King"), "And thus God breaketh the bands of death, having gained the victory over death" (Mosiah 15:8).

Likewise, only a God could satisfy the demands of justice. "Unto every kingdom is given a law" (D&C 88:3), and unto every law, there is a punishment affixed (2 Nephi 2:26). And "justice claimeth the creature and executeth the law . . . if not so, the works of justice would be destroyed, and God would cease to be God" (Alma 42:22).

This is no idle threat. As discussed in chapter 11, God's power flows from willing obeisance and worship of lesser intelligences (D&C 29:36). If God were to violate the law of justice, there would be no basis for trust in His word, and God would cease to be God. "But God ceaseth not to be God, and mercy claimeth the penitent and mercy cometh because of the Atonement" (Alma 42:23). Before the Savior's agony ended, the elements groaned and the lesser intelligences affirmed that the suffering of Jesus Christ was sufficient to satisfy the demands of justice, absorbing the full punishment of the law (1 Nephi 19:12; Matthew 27:51, 54; Moses 7:55–56).

Only a God could descend into the furthest depths of perdition where "the very jaws of hell [gaped] open the mouth wide after [him]" (D&C 122:7). He "who did no sin" sank lower than the most benighted souls of all human history, descending "below them all" (D&C 122:8). In the wisdom of God, "The end, the width, the height, the depth, and the misery [of hell]" no man can understand, "except those who are ordained unto this condemnation" (D&C 76:48). But Jesus Christ understands. He knows the dimensions of hell by personal experience, because he, a God, was "ordained unto this condemnation" that we might not suffer if we would repent (D&C 19:16).

Infinite suffering endured by an infinite being [God]; and still we ponder: "Lord, how is it done?" Or as the woman on the radio program insinuated, "How could the Atonement with all it entailed be worked out in just a few hours of Christ's mortal life?"

The short answer is: It couldn't! Like the servant of Elijah, we must pray that the Lord will open our eyes to a larger reality. While Jesus Christ suffered very real, unfathomable agony from the anguish of Gethsemane to the cruelty of the cross, the ultimate victory over death and sin could only be worked out under conditions where the limits of suffering and the flow of time pose no constraints.

As the Only Begotten Son of the Father after the manner of the flesh and as the Creator of heaven and earth whose voice the elements obey, Jesus Christ was uniquely endowed with power to determine the time and conditions of His own death. He taught, "For as the Father hath life in himself; so hath he given to the Son to have life in himself" (John 5:26). "No man taketh [my life] from me, but I lay it down of myself. I have power to lay it down, and I have power to take it again" (John 10:18). Accordingly, the Savior was able to keep His spirit united with His body while transcending the limits of mortal suffering until the crushing demands of justice were fully absorbed. How exquisite His pain? He alone can know—beyond mortal capacity to experience or conceptualize. From any mortal perspective: Infinite!

As for the element of time, Jehovah God created it, but is not bound by it (Neal A. Maxwell, *Plain and Precious Things*, 57). Even in this mortal state, the Creator possessed power to escape the constraints of linear time and access the eternal now, where all things past, present, and future are continually before His eyes (Moses 1:6; D&C 38:2). In a similar state, Moses was shown "the earth, yea, all of it; and there was not a particle of it which he did not behold . . . And he beheld also the inhabitants thereof, and there was not a soul which he beheld not" (Moses 1:27–28). In a brief lapse of time, Moses perceived and comprehended billions and billions of individual souls and every composite of element that makes up our earthly home. In similar manner, Jesus Christ beheld and comprehended each of us personally and all our transgressions, individually and collectively, throughout all His creations as He atoned for humankind.

Like a magnifying glass that focuses diffused light into a concentrated point, the cumulative anguish of all our sins, sicknesses, and sufferings through all eternity, accessed simultaneously in the eternal now, bore down upon the Savior of worlds. No finite mind can stretch to imagine, let alone understand, the intense agony He endured in the garden and again on the cross. It is precisely because the price He paid is so beyond our capacity to comprehend that it is fittingly denominated: infinite.

And how long did He suffer under this infinite load? The answer lies in the relationship of linear time to the eternal now. How long is six hours, twelve hours, or twenty-four hours as marked on earth in the eternal now where time is no more? The answer is the same for each increment of time. It is an eternity! An infinite load borne for an eternity—surely it was an infinite sacrifice.

When Enos asked, "How is it done?" The Lord answered, "Because of thy faith in Christ . . . wherefore, go to, thy faith hath made thee whole" (Enos 1:7–8). The Atonement of Jesus Christ, worked out from the foundation of the world, requires faith, both then and now, to believe one lone figure paid for all sins, bore all infirmities, overpowered death, fully satisfied the demands of justice, and descended below all things. Given the incalculable requirements, it is not difficult to imagine that one of the inducements used by Lucifer in our premortal state to persuade one-third of the hosts of heaven to follow Him is that the Atonement was impossible, even for a God. One-third of the Father's children simply would not believe Jesus Christ could drain the bitter dregs from the cup of "God's wrath" and satisfy the full extent of the law.

In this constrained world with our finite minds, mortal humans will never fully comprehend the infinite Atonement, but our faith is fully capable of accessing its eternal reality and endless power. Just as Enos "knew that God could not lie; wherefore [his] guilt was swept away" (Enos 1:6), we can feel a peace that surpasses all understanding and know the supernal goodness of His infinite Atonement in our lives.

In the economy of God, one truth stands above all others: Jesus Christ is Lord, Savior, and Redeemer of all humankind. He was the Lamb slain from the foundation of the world. He has "graven us on the palms of his hands" (Isaiah 49:16) through His infinite Atonement, and still His arms are outstretched to all who will exercise faith in His name unto repentance. Through all eons of time, His atoning sacrifice stands supreme. "Father, behold the sufferings and death of Him who did no sin, in whom thou wast well pleased" (D&C 45:4). In deepest humility and overflowing gratitude, we can rest assured: "Lord, it is done!"

# AFTERWORD

CHAPTER 17

# HOW I KNOW

So we return to Mark Twain's witty observation that what gets us into trouble is cleaving to things "that just ain't so" (Goodreads.com). With your indulgence, I would like to close this incomplete exploration of God's economy by sharing a personal journey that provides my answer to the question: How do you know that things in the economy of God are true and not just things that "ain't so"?

I grew up in a loving home, the fifth of six boys with no girls. In my family, no one ever complained about what was for dinner. It was take it or leave it. There were too many hungry mouths more than willing to consume my portion and theirs too. It was survival of the fittest.

Dinner was often accompanied by lively discussion. We regularly debated everything from politics and religion to science, human nature, and the philosophies of men. In those family discussions, I learned to question everything. As I approached my mid-teens, two of my older brothers had stayed close to the Church and gone on to serve missions, but two had not. At sixteen, I was deeply skeptical of all religion and doubted the existence of God.

One night, I found myself in the company of a young woman. The conversation somehow turned to religion, and I shared many of my questions and concerns with her. She listened patiently and then said, "You know, Dwight, I have many of those same questions, and I don't know most of the answers. But this is what I know: When I do what is taught in the Church, I am happy; and when I don't, I am not."

Being the self-styled rationalist and empiricist that I am, two aspects of her response struck me. First, I could test her proposition in my own life. I did not have to accept the assertions of others. Though only sixteen, I had experience enough to test the validity of her statement. Second, if the proposition were true, it struck me that it was probably not by chance. If true, there was likely a higher power that designed the world to be so, in which case He had revealed His designs and purposes to leaders who, in turn, imparted these truths to others.

I pondered this proposition for the better part of two weeks, sifting through specific incidents in my life with an honest, searching heart and testing this idea as thoroughly and objectively as I could. At the end of those two weeks, I concluded my friend was correct. Of course, my realization did not produce an immediate testimony in me, but at sixteen, I began to pray with faith and real intent.

Almost immediately, I noticed an increase of peace and quiet joy in my life. In time, as I prayed more earnestly, sweet answers came, borne of the spirit. I realized that God was listening to and answering my prayers. I felt His guiding hand in my life, giving me confidence that I was on a good path. I also sensed greater purpose and direction in my daily life. Then one evening as I knelt in prayer, I was wrapped in a glorious and enlivening warmth. It came in a most unexpected yet powerful way, full of peace and light, providing a profound witness that energized my whole being. Other experiences borne of the Spirit followed, and my testimony of God and of His plan for me and for all His children grew.

At age nineteen, I was called to serve a mission. In retrospect, I see that my mission was the most shaping experience of my life. I had many profound spiritual experiences on my mission, including casting out Satan, administering healing blessings, experiencing the gift of tongues, foretelling future events, and receiving personal revelation with great power. In addition, while interacting with people from all walks of life, I saw firsthand the results of good and bad choices. I saw the devastation and heartache of adultery and the insecurity and complications arising from premarital sexual relations. I saw the blessings of getting a good education, of being honest in all one's dealings, and of serving others generously. I observed the power of family, both good and bad, to bless lives or produce lifelong challenges for individuals. I saw the crippling curse of addictions and the empty lives of people searching for something but not knowing where to look for purpose or hope.

I also saw imperfect people striving to change. I witnessed investigators being taught correct principles and then having the courage and faith to apply these principles in their lives. I beheld the power of repentance and obedience to God's teachings, which produced an increase in the fruits of the spirit as described by the Apostle Paul: love, joy, peace, long-suffering, gentleness, goodness, faith, meekness, and temperance (Galatians 5:22–23), and these fruits were all good.

What I really witnessed is the wisdom of an all-powerful, all-loving God who created this world with both physical and moral laws. Surely "There is a law, irrevocably decreed in heaven before the foundations of this world, upon which all blessings are predicated. And when we obtain any blessing from God, it is by obedience to that law upon which it is predicated" (D&C 130:20–21).

Later, as my wife and I raised our five children, we tried to emphasize, "Do this, and it will bless your life." It is most comforting to know, in advance, certain seeds will grow and begin to be delicious to the souls of our children, because the Church of Jesus Christ teaches the laws upon which all blessings are predicated.

As members of the Lord's Church, we realize we have no corner on access to blessings that flow from obedience to correct principles and laws. Because they are laws established by a loving God, correct principles bless the lives of people of all faiths, along with those of no particular faith.

Without a doubt, the most powerful testimony of tithing I have ever heard was borne by a woman of no particular faith. She noticed this important principle while reading her Bible. She spent an inordinate amount of time researching charitable organizations to learn which ones would get her money most effectively to those whose lives she wanted to bless. She told me of how her business had prospered and her life had filled with happiness since she had begun to pay 10 percent of her gross income to support charitable organizations. She stated that she would never think of not paying 10 percent of her income, because it had produced such blessings in her life.

Likewise, the sweetest description I have yet encountered of the joy that accompanies Sabbath day worship came from a book written by a devout Jew, Hermann Wouk, in *This Is My God*. Wouk wrote, "If one were to ask me what I love most about my Jewish faith, I would answer without hesitation: 'the Sabbath'" (*This Is My God*, 41). He then went on to describe how the Sabbath is filled with worship and family, reflection and scripture reading—all producing joy and setting it apart from every other day of the week.

Testifying of the effects of God's laws, on September 17, 1859, in Dayton, Ohio, Abraham Lincoln inscribed the following words in a Bible belonging to Miss Annie Harries: "Live by the words within these covers and you will be forever happy" (Daniel Mark Epstein, *The Lincolns: Portrait of A Marriage*, 236).

Knowing that these laws operate unfailingly, do we take full advantage of the powerful gifts and blessings provided by the Lord and taught by church leaders? Do we regularly feel the joy of Family Home Evening, of ministering in the homes of others, of complying with the Word of Wisdom, tithing, and temple worthiness? Have you recently felt the joy of praying so long that you did not want to cease? When was the last time you read the scriptures so regularly and in such depth that you couldn't wait to immerse yourself in them again? Have you gone through the temple recently and felt the power of the temple going through you? Have you sensed, in wonder and awe, the supernal goodness of God, proclaiming in your soul as Moses did, "Now for this cause I know that man is nothing, which thing I never had supposed" (Moses 1:10)?

I stand before my Savior today a flawed and imperfect man. As I reflect back through my years in mortality, I know my life has been blessed with peace and joy to the degree that I have conformed to the teachings of the gospel. Conversely, my joy has been diminished when I have strayed from God's laws: "Wickedness never was happiness" (Alma 41:10).

Humbly, I bear my witness to all who will hear. I know God lives. He is the father of our spirits. He loves us with a perfect love. I know Jesus is the Christ, my personal Savior and yours. He has purchased our souls with His precious blood. I know Joseph Smith was His prophet, an instrument in the hands of God to restore His true Church with priesthood authority that binds on earth that which shall be bound in heaven (Matthew 18:18) and to bring forth the Book of Mormon, a second testament of Jesus Christ. I know that Jesus Christ himself leads us through living prophets, seers, and revelators. The glorious gospel of Jesus Christ is not only the plan of salvation and the plan of redemption. It is also the plan of happiness and joy. It was so in our premortal existence. It is in this life and will be in the life to come.

The longer I live, the more I realize how few things I really know, but I know these few things deep in my soul. I know them by the power of the Spirit, witnessed to my soul on multiple occasions. I know them by observation of the operation of God's laws in my life and in the lives of others. Of these precious truths, I humbly bear witness to all who will hear. Glory be to God the Father and to His Son, Jesus Christ, now and forever. Amen.

# BIBLIOGRAPHY

Adams, John. BrainyQuote.com. See brainyquote.com/quotes/john_adams_134175. Accessed March 17, 2020.

Boaz, David. "The Man Who Would Not Be King." Washington, DC: Cato Institute, Feb. 20, 2006.

Callister, Tad R. *The Infinite Atonement.* Salt Lake City: Deseret Book, 2000.

Campbell, Beverly. *Eve and the Choice Made in Eden.* Salt Lake City: Bookcraft, 2003.

Christofferson, D. Todd. "The Power of Covenants." *Ensign,* May 2009.

_____. "The Resurrection of Jesus Christ." *Ensign,* May 2014.

Clark, Douglas E. *The Blessings of Abraham.* American Fork, UT: Covenant Communications, 2005.

Drummond, Henry. *Natural Law in the Spiritual World.* New York: J. Pott, 1887.

Epstein, Daniel Mark. *The Lincolns: Portrait of a Marriage.* New York: Ballantine Books (Random House), 2009.

Faust, James E., Jan Pinborough, and Michael F. Moody. "This Is the Christ." Salt Lake City: The Church of Jesus Christ of Latter-day Saints, 1995.

*Fiddler on the Roof*. Film produced and directed by Norman Jewison. New York: Mirisch Corporation, 1971.

Gaskill, Alonzo L. *The Lost Language of Symbolism*. Salt Lake City: Deseret Book, 2003.

Givens, Terryl L., and Fiona Givens. *The God Who Weeps*. Salt Lake City: Ensign Peak, 2012.

Goldman, William. *The Princess Bride*. Film produced by Andrew Scheinman and directed by Rob Reiner, 1987. See Goodreads.com, goodreads.com/quotes/341708-inconceivable-you-keep-using-that-word-i-do-not-think. Accessed March 17, 2020.

*Gospel Principles*. Salt Lake City: The Church of Jesus Christ of Latter-day Saints, 2011.

Habermas, Gary R., and Michael R. Licona. *The Case for the Resurrection of Jesus*. Grand Rapids, MI: Kregel Publications, 2004.

Hardy, Benjamin P. "Quotes That Will Reshape Your Life." *Huffington Post*. See huffpost.com/entry/2-quotes-that-will-reshape-your-approach-to-life_b_58b44d75e4b0e5fdf6197505, February 27, 2017. Accessed March 19, 2020.

Hill, Napoleon. Goodreads.com. See goodreads.com/quotes/536677-the-strongest-oak-of-the-forest-is-not-the-one. Accessed March 20, 2020.

_____. *Law of Success*, 21st century edition. New York: The Penguin Group, 2008.

_____. *Think and Grow Rich*. New York: Fawcett Crest, 1960.

Hinckley, Gordon B. "The Symbol of Christ." *New Era*, April 1990.

Holland, Jeffrey. Singles conference address (unpublished). Palo Alto, California, March 2013, as recorded by Marianne Monson.

Hugo, Victor. *Les Miserables*. New York: New American Library (Penguin Group), 2013.

*Hymns of The Church of Jesus Christ of Latter-day Saints*. Salt Lake City: Deseret Book, 1985.

Isaacson, Walter. *Einstein, His Life and Universe.* New York: Simon and Schuster, 2007.

Jeppson, Peter. Know Your Religion Lecture Series (audiotape). Provo, UT: Brigham Young University/The Church of Jesus Christ of Latter-day Saints, February 1977.

Johnson, Paul. *George Washington: The Founding Father.* New York: HarperCollins, 2005.

*Journal of Discourses.* 26 vols. London: Latter-day Saints' Book Depot, 1854–86.

Jung, C. G. *Nietzsche's Zarathustra.* Princeton, NJ: Princeton University Press, 1988.

Kimball, Spencer W. *The Miracle of Forgiveness.* Salt Lake City: Bookcraft, 1969.

Lewis, C. S. *Mere Christianity.* New York: Simon and Schuster, 1996.

Lings, Martin. *Muhammad, His Life Based on the Earliest Sources.* Rochester, VT: Inner Traditions, 2006.

"Little Miracle: The Lesson of the Moth." Fatherduffy.com, August 28, 2019. See fatherduffy.com/helping-a-moth/. Accessed March 17, 2020.

Lowry, Mark, and Buddy Greene. "Mary, Did You Know?" 1984. Azlyrics.com. See azlyrics.com/lyrics/pentatonix/marydidyouknow.html. Accessed March 20, 2020.

Madsen, Truman G. *Christ and the Inner Life.* Salt Lake City: Bookcraft, 1988.

_____. *Joseph Smith the Prophet.* Salt Lake City: Bookcraft, 1989.

Maxwell, Neal A. "A More Determined Discipleship." *Ensign*, February 1979.

_____. *All These Things Shall Give Thee Experience.* Salt Lake City: Deseret Book, 1980.

_____. *Not My Will But Thine.* Salt Lake City: Bookcraft, 1988.

_____. *Plain and Precious Things*. Salt Lake City: Deseret Book, 1983.

_____. *Things As They Really Are*. Salt Lake City: Deseret Book, 1978.

*Miracle on Ice*. Film directed by Gavin O'Connor and produced by Mark Ciardi. Walt Disney Productions, 2004. Wikipedia. See en.wikipedia.org/wiki/Miracle_on_Ice. Accessed March 20, 2020.

Monson, Dwight E. *Shared Beliefs, Honest Differences*. Bountiful, UT: Horizon, 1998.

Nelson, Russell M. "The Atonement." *Ensign,* November 1996.

Neuenschwander, Dennis B. "Holy Place, Sacred Space." *Ensign*, May 2003.

Packer, Boyd K. "The Candle of the Lord." *Ensign,* January 1983.

_____. "Touch of the Master's Hand." *Ensign*, May 2001.

*Passion of Christ, The*. Film produced by Bruce Davey, Mel Gibson, and Stephen McEveety. Directed by Mel Gibson. 2004.

Pontius, John. *Visions of Glory*. Springville, Utah: Cedar Fort, 2012.

Roberts, B. H. *The Mormon Doctrine of Deity*. Bountiful, UT: Horizon, 1982.

Schuon, Firthjof. *Understanding Islam*. Bloomington, IN: World Wisdom Books, 1998.

Sleeth, Natalie. "Were You There on That Christmas Night?" Carol Stream, ILL: Hope Publishing, 1976.

Smith, Huston. *The Religions of Man*. New York: Harper Perennial, 1992.

Smith, Joseph. *Lectures on Faith*. Salt Lake City: Deseret Book, 1985.

_____. *Teachings of the Prophet Joseph Smith*. Selected by Joseph Fielding Smith. Salt Lake City: Deseret Book, 1970.

Stansberry, Porter. *Stansberry's Investment Advisory*. September 12, 2012.

Twain, Mark. Goodreads.com. See goodreads.com/quotes/738123-what-gets-us-into-trouble-is-not-what-we-don-t. Accessed March 17, 2020.

Van Biema, David. "Mother Teresa's Crisis of Faith." *Time Magazine,* Aug. 23, 2007.

*Words of Joseph Smith, The.* Compiled by Andrew F. Ehat and Lyndon W. Cook. Salt Lake City: Bookcraft, 1981.

Wilcox, Brad. *The Continuous Atonement.* Salt Lake City: Deseret Book, 2009.

World Series. Los Angeles Dodgers vs. Oakland Athletics, 1988. Scoresreport.com. See scoresreport.com/2018/11/05/i-dont-believe-what-i-just-saw-jack-buck-and-the-greatest-call-in-baseball-history/. Accessed March 20, 2020.

Wouk, Herman. *This Is My God.* New York: Doubleday, Doran, and Company, 1935.

# NOTES

# NOTES

# NOTES

# NOTES

# Notes

# NOTES

# About the Author

Dwight Monson graduated with honors from Harvard University and with an MBA from Stanford Graduate School of Management. He is the author of *Shared Beliefs, Honest Differences: A Biblical Basis for Comparing the Doctrines of Mormons and Other Christians*, and *Understanding the LDS Temple: Experiencing God's Love*.

Dwight was a senior partner in a major U.S. consulting firm, specializing in health care, where he cofounded Mission-Based Management—an approach endorsed and sponsored by the Association of American Medical Colleges for managing schools of medicine. He was a frequent speaker at national health care meetings and seminars. He has also authored numerous professional publications.

Dwight currently resides in St. George, Utah, with his beloved wife, Marilynn Allred, where they cofounded "Dixie's Got Talent," an annual celebration of local talent that has raised need-based scholarships for more than one hundred students at Dixie State University.